Holiday CROCHET

Holiday CROCHET

FABULOUS FESTIVE PROJECTS FOR WREATHS, HOME ACCESSORIES, DECORATIONS, AND MORE

Kate Eastwood

CICO BOOKS

Published in 2026 by CICO Books
An imprint of Ryland Peters & Small Ltd
1452 Davis Bugg Road,
Warrenton, NC 27589

www.rylandpeters.com

10 9 8 7 6 5 4 3 2 1

The projects in this book originally featured in *Crocheted Wreaths & Garlands*, *Crocheted Home*, *Crochet with Flowers and Plants*, *Introduction to Crochet*, and *Crocheted Squares*.

US Library of Congress CIP data has been applied for.

ISBN: 978-1-80065-650-5

Printed in China

Photographers: Emma Mitchell and James Gardiner
Stylist: Nel Haynes
Pattern checkers: Carol Ibbetson and Jemima Bicknell
Illustrator: Stephen Dew
Editor: Marie Clayton

Editorial assistant: Danielle Rawlings
Designer: Paul Stradling
Senior designer: Emily Breen
Art director: Sally Powell
Head of production: Patricia Harrington
Publisher: Carmel Edmonds

Contents

Introduction

Little did I know when I tentatively started to teach myself to crochet by watching YouTube videos a few years back, that it would become such a big part of my day-to-day life. I can honestly say that it is very rare for me to have a day when I don't crochet.

There are three chapters in this book: **Wreaths and Decorations** has everything you need to turn your home into a winter wonderland, with mini Christmas trees (page 43), a holly wreath complete with gold birds (page 21), and a mistletoe string (page 26). Next, **For The Home** features makes that you can bring out year after year, from a pompom pillow (page 54) to frosted ivy-leaf coasters (page 78) and a starry basket (page 64) that's perfect for storing presents. Finally, **Cards and Gifts** includes patterns to help you make thoughtful and unique presents, such as pretty candle jars that make lovely table favors (page 106), and stunning Christmas-, Hanukkah-, and Diwali- themed squares (page 97, 103, and 112) that can be used in a variety of different makes such as wall art, greetings cards, collages, and garlands (see page 126). It's entirely up to you!

If you are new to crochet, turn to the Techniques section on pages 115–126 and the Abbreviations on page 127. Each project has a skill rating, from Easy (one circle) to Intermediate (two circles) and Advanced (three circles). Start with the Easy patterns then move on to the next two levels once you know the basic techniques.

I've included approximate finished measurements for each project, but keep in mind these may vary slightly depending on the yarn you use. For example, if you substitute light worsted (DK) for the fingering (4-ply) yarn I used, the project will be slightly larger. Likewise, if you use fingering instead of light worsted, the finished piece will be a bit smaller. If you're using a different yarn weight, you might need to adjust your hook size accordingly, but don't worry—this will only affect the final size slightly.

I very much hope that this will become a book that you can dip into for festive ideas and inspiration—something that really helps you get into the holiday spirit!

CHAPTER 1

Wreaths and DECORATIONS

Wish Upon a Star Wreath

Whether for a child's bedroom or as an addition to your Christmas decorations, this wreath is designed with simplicity and understatement in mind. The three different-sized stars have been added to a dark twig wreath to make them stand out for full effect. To give each star extra twinkle, a strand of metallic thread has been worked in with the yarn.

Wreath

LARGE STAR

(make 2 in A, 1 in B)

Round 1: Using A or B held tog with C, make a magic ring, 5sc into the ring. Work in a continuous spiral. PM in last st and move up as each round is finished.

Round 2: 2sc in each st to end. *(10 sts)*

Round 3: *1sc, 2sc in next st; rep from * 4 more times, sl st in first st to join. *(15 sts)*

Round 4: *Ch7, sl st in second ch from hook, 1sc, 1hdc, 2dc in next ch, miss last 2 ch and next 2 sts of center, sl st in next st; rep from * 4 more times around (5 points), ending last point with sl st in base of first point.

Fasten off.

MEDIUM STAR

(make 4 in A, 4 in B)

Round 1: Using A or B held tog with C, make a magic ring, 5sc into the ring. Work in a continuous spiral, do not join.

Round 2: 2sc in each st to end, sl st in first st to join. *(10 sts)*

Round 3: *Ch5, sl st in second ch from hook, 1sc, 1hdc, miss last ch and next st of center, sl st in next st; rep from * 4 more times around (5 points), ending last point with sl st in base of first point.

Fasten off.

SMALL STAR

(make 3 in A, 2 in B)

Round 1: Using A or B held tog with C, make a magic ring, 5sc into the ring, sl st in first st to join.

Round 2: *Ch4, sl st in second ch from hook, 1sc, miss last ch, sl st in next st of center; rep from * 4 more times around (5 points), ending last point with sl st in base of first point.

Fasten off.

Making up and finishing

Block the stars. Lay the wreath on a flat surface. Use blocking pins to position the blocked stars where you want them to be. Glue firmly in place with a hot glue gun.

To finish off the wreath, add a bow in a coordinating color by attaching it with a glue gun.

SKILL LEVEL •

YARN AND MATERIALS

James C. Brett Twinkle (3% polyester, 97% acrylic) light worsted (DK) weight yarn, 328yd (300m) per 3½oz (100g) ball

1 ball in each of:
Silver shade TK8 (A)
White shade TK2 (B)

Drops Glitter Thread, 765yd (700m) per ½oz (10g) spool

1 spool of Silver shade 02 (C)

12in (30cm) diameter twig wreath

Coordinating ribbon

HOOKS AND EQUIPMENT

US size B/1 (2mm) crochet hook

Stitch marker

Pins

Hot glue gun

FINISHED MEASUREMENTS

Each large star: approx. 2¼in (5.5cm) wide

Wreath: 12in (30cm) diameter

GAUGE (TENSION)

15 sts x 15 rows = 2¼in (6cm) square working single crochet, using a US size B/1 (2mm) crochet hook.

ABBREVIATIONS

See page 127.

TIP

To give your wreath a more festive feel, use a red glitter yarn such as James C. Brett Twinkle in a red shade, to make the stars.

Wishing on
a star...

Winter Garland

There is something very special about the first winter frost, the sparkle that it brings to the smallest of things, and the delicious crunch underfoot. This winter garland aims to catch all of those feelings within its silver gray oak leaves, winter acorns, and shimmering stars.

SKILL LEVEL ●●●

YARN AND MATERIALS

King Cole Baby Glitz (97% acrylic, 3% polyester) light worsted (DK) weight yarn, approx. 317yd (290m) per 3½oz (100g) ball

1 ball each of shades:
Silver 3093 (A)
Diamond White 483 (B)
Cream 105 (C)

HOOKS AND EQUIPMENT

US size C/2–D/3 (3mm) crochet hook

Stitch marker

Polyester toy stuffing

2 lengths of 1¾oz (50g) gray raffia

Florist's wire

Needle and matching thread

Coordinating ribbon for bows

FINISHED MEASUREMENTS

Each oak leaf: 3½in (9cm) long

Each star: 2in (5cm) from point to opposite point

Each completed acorn: 1½in (3.5cm)

Garland: approx. 43¼in (110cm) long

GAUGE (TENSION)

15 sts x 15 rows = 2¾ x 2½in (7 x 6.5cm) working single crochet, using a US size C/2–D/3 (3mm) crochet hook.

ABBREVIATIONS

See page 127.

For the garland

OAK LEAF

(make 13)

Using A, ch14.

Round 1: 1sc in 2nd ch from hook, 1sc in each of next 3 ch, 1hdc in each of next 5 ch, 1dc in each of next 3 ch, 5dc in last ch, do not turn, working back down other side of ch, 1dc in each of next 5 ch, 1hdc in each of next 4 ch, 1sc in each of last 3 ch, join with a sl st in first st.

Round 2:

Lobe 1: 2sc in first st, sl st in next st, (1sc, 1hdc, 1dc) in next st, sl st in next st.

Lobe 2: Sl st in next st, (1sc, 1hdc, 1dc) in next st, sl st in next st.

Lobe 3: Sl st in next st, (1sc, 1hdc, 2dc) in next st, sl st in next st.

Lobe 4: Sl st in next st, (1sc, 1hdc, 2dc) in next st, sl st in next st.

Lobe 5: Sl st in next st, (1sc, 1hdc, 1dc) in next st, (1dc, 1hdc, 1sc) in next st, sl st in each of next 2 sts.

Lobe 6: (Ch2, 1dc, 1hdc) in same st as sl st, (1hdc, 1sc) in next st, sl st in next st.

Lobe 7: Ch2, (1dc, 1hdc, sl st) in next st, sl st in next st.

Lobe 8: (Sl st, ch2) in next st, (1dc, 1hdc) in next st, (1hdc, 1sc) in next st, sl st in next st.

Lobe 9: (Sl st, ch1) in next st, 2hdc in next st, 1sc, sl st in next st.

Sl st in base of leaf, ch5, sl st in each of 5 ch, sl st in base of leaf.
Fasten off.

ACORN CUP

(make 13)

Round 1: Using C, make a magic ring, 5sc into the ring.
Work in a continuous spiral. PM in last st and move up as each round is finished.
Round 2: 2sc in each st to end. 10 sts.
Round 3: *1sc, 2sc in next st; rep from * to end. 15 sts.
Round 4: *1sc in each of next 2 sts, 2sc in next st; rep from * to end. 20 sts.
Round 5: *1sc in each of next 2 sts, sc2tog: rep to end, join with a sl st in first st. 15 sts.
Fasten off.

ACORN

(make 13)

Round 1: Using B, make a magic ring, 4sc into the ring.
Work in a continuous spiral. PM in last st and move up as each round is finished.
Round 2: 2sc in each st to end. 8 sts.
Round 3: *1sc, 2sc in next st; rep from * to end. 12 sts.
Rounds 4 to 7: 1sc in each st to end.
Fasten off.

STAR

(make 6)

Round 1: Using C, make a magic ring, 5sc into the ring.
Work in a continuous spiral, do not join.
Round 2: 2sc in each st to end, join with a sl st in first st. 10 sts.
Round 3: *Ch5, sl st in 2nd ch from hook, 1sc, 1hdc, miss last ch and next st of central circle, sl st in next st; rep from * 4 times around (5 points), ending last point with sl st in base of first point.
Fasten off.

Making up and finishing

Stuff each acorn, then place it inside a cup and stitch in place.
Fasten off.
Make the raffia wreath base as explained on page 125. Lay your raffia base on a flat surface and use blocking pins to position your leaves, acorns, and stars where you want them to be.
Stitch them all securely in place by sewing them onto the raffia using a needle and thread.
Add a bow in a coordinating ribbon at each end of the garland.
Tie small string loops at the back of the garland for hanging.

Tabletop Christmas Tree

Standing at just over 16in (40cm) tall, this miniature tree, in its own terracotta pot, will adorn any table or corner of your home. Whether left in all its simplicity of natural greens or decorated with a string of tiny white lights, it offers a beautiful festive touch for any small space and would also make a lovely gift.

For the tree

Work in a continuous spiral from Round 2 onward, from top down. PM at end of each round and move up as each round is finished.

The tree is worked in loop st using two strands of yarn.

Using a US size J/10 (6mm) hook and 1 strand each of A and B held together, make a magic ring.

Round 1: 8sc into ring, sl st in beg st to join, turn. *(8 sts)*

Work in loop st from now onward.

Round 2: [1sc, 2sc in next st] 4 times. *(12 sts)*

Round 3: 12 sc.

Round 4: [2sc, 2sc in next st] 4 times. *(16 sts)*

Round 5: 16sc.

Round 6: [3sc, 2sc in next st] 4 times. *(20 sts)*

Round 7: 20sc.

Round 8: [4sc, 2sc in next st] 4 times. *(24 sts)*

Round 9: 24sc.

Round 10: [5sc, 2sc in next st] 4 times. *(28 sts)*

Round 11: 28sc.

Round 12: [6sc, 2sc in next st] 4 times. *(32 sts)*

Round 13: 32sc.

Round 14: [7sc, 2sc in next st] 4 times. *(36 sts)*

Round 15: 36sc.

Round 16: [8sc, 2sc in next st] 4 times. *(40 sts)*

SKILL LEVEL ●●

YARN AND MATERIALS

Cascade Yarns 220 Superwash (100% merino wool) light worsted (DK) weight yarn, 219yd (200m) per 3½oz (100g) ball

1 ball in each of:

Peridot 286 (A)

Turtle 1919 (B)

Rico Creative Lamé (62% polyester, 38% polyamide) sport (4-ply) weight yarn, 148yd (135m) per 1¾oz (50g) ball

1 ball of Gold 002 (C)

Toy stuffing

16¼in (41cm) long branch, approx. 1in (2.5cm) wide, as straight as possible

Small flowerpot: 3¾in (9.5cm) diameter, 3in (7.5cm) high

Floral foam

Moss

20in (50cm) of ribbon, ⅜in (1cm) wide

HOOKS AND EQUIPMENT

US size J/10 (6mm) and US size C/2–D/3 (3mm) crochet hooks

Stitch marker

Yarn needle

Hot glue gun

FINISHED MEASUREMENTS

Tree height: 16¼in (41cm)

Width at base of tree: 7½in (19cm)

Star: 2¾ x 2¾in (7 x 7cm)

GAUGE (TENSION)

Exact gauge (tension) is not essential on this project.

ABBREVIATIONS

See page 127.

SPECIAL ABBREVIATIONS

loop st: wrap yarn over index finger to make loop, insert hook in next st, take hook over top of yarn at front of finger and then back under yarn at back of finger, leaving loop on finger, pull hook through, leaving 2 sts on hook, adjust loop size on finger if necessary, yoh, pull through all sts on hook and remove finger from loop.

Round 17: 40sc.
Round 18: [9sc, 2sc in next st] 4 times. *(44 sts)*
Round 19: 44sc.
Round 20: [10sc, 2sc in next st] 4 times. *(48 sts)*
Rounds 21 and 22: 48sc.
Round 23: [11sc, 2sc in next st] 4 times. *(52 sts)*
Rounds 24 and 25: 52sc.
Round 26: [12sc, 2sc in next st] 4 times. *(56 sts)*
Rounds 27 to 29: 56sc, sl st in next st.
Fasten off and sew in ends.
Add circle of glue to top of branch with hot glue gun. Place branch inside tree, sticking top of branch to inside top of tree. Turn tree and stem upside down and stuff tree fully, working around central branch.
Round 30: With tree upside down, 56scBLO in sts of Round 29. *(56 sts)*
Round 31: [2sc, sc2tog] 14 times. *(42 sts)*
Round 32: [1sc, sc2tog] 14 times. *(28 sts)*
Round 33: [1sc, sc2tog] 9 times, 1sc. *(19 sts)*
Round 34: [1sc, sc2tog] 6 times, 1sc. *(13 sts)*
If necessary, cont working rounds of decreasing as set until opening is tight around stem.
Fasten off and sew in ends.

For the star

(make 2)
Work in a continuous spiral to end Round 3, PM at end of each round and move up as each round is finished.
Using a US size C/2-D/3 (3mm) hook and C, make a magic ring.
Round 1: 5sc into ring. *(5 sts)*
Round 2: [2sc in next st] 5 times. *(10 sts)*
Round 3: [1sc, 2sc in next st] 5 times, sl st in beg st to join. *(15 sts)*
Round 4: *Ch7, sl st in second ch from hook, 1sc, 1hdc, 1dc, 1tr, 1ttr, skip 2 sts from Round 3, sl st in next st; rep from * 3 more times to make 4 more points, sl st in beg st to join.
Fasten off.

Making up and finishing

Place the two star pieces WS together and join with a single crochet seam. At each point, ch3, sl st back in first ch. Before joining completely, stuff the star lightly. Finish closing up, fasten off, and sew in the ends.
Fill the flowerpot with floral foam and make an indent in the center where the branch will go.
Carefully push the tree down into the floral foam so that it is standing firmly. Use the hot glue to add a layer of glue over the top of the foam to help the tree to stay firm. Cover the glue with moss.
Use the glue gun to stick the star to the top of the tree.
Tie the ribbon around the top of the pot, adding a dot of glue under the ribbon to keep it in place.

Stars and Trees Garland

Christmas trees come in all shapes and sizes—and these miniature ones are the perfect size to be strung on some bright cord and hung along a shelf or fireplace throughout the festive season. As a bright color contrast, glittering red stars hang between each tree.

SKILL LEVEL ●●●

YARN AND MATERIALS

Rico Ricorumi Twinkly Twinkly (99% cotton, 1% polyester) light worsted (DK) weight yarn, approx. 62yd (57m) per ⅞oz (25g) ball
4 balls of Red 009 (A)

Rico Baby Cotton Soft (50% cotton, 50% acrylic) light worsted (DK) weight yarn, approx. 136yd (125m) per 1¾oz (50g) ball
2 balls each of shades:
Alga 084 (B)
Mint 031 (C)
Ice 051 (D)

Anchor Artiste Metallic (80% viscose, 20% polyester) thread, approx. 109yd (100m) per ⅞oz (25g) ball
1 ball each of shades:
Gold 300 (E)
Red 318 (F)

Polyester toy stuffing

Thin string for hanging loops

70in (175cm) red cord

Coordinating ribbon for bows

HOOKS AND EQUIPMENT

US size C/2-D/3 (3mm) and US size B/1 (2mm) crochet hooks

Stitch marker

Needle and matching thread

FINISHED MEASUREMENTS

Each tree: 5¼in (13cm) high

Each large star: 2½in (6.5cm)

Each small star: ¾in (2cm)

Garland: approx. 54in (135cm) long

GAUGE (TENSION)

15 sts x 15 rows = 2¾ x 2½in (7 x 6.5cm) working single crochet, using a US size C/2-D/3 (3mm) crochet hook and Rico Ricorumi Twinkly Twinkly.

ABBREVIATIONS

See page 127.

For the garland

TREE

(make 3 in B, 4 in C with base in D)

Make the base:

Round 1: Using D and US size C/2-D/3 (3mm) hook, make a magic ring, 6sc into the ring.
Round 2: 2sc in each st to end, join with a sl st in first st. *(12 sts)*
Round 3: Ch1, 12sc BLO, join with a sl st in first st.
Rounds 4 to 8: Ch1, working in both loops as normal, 1sc in each st to end, join with a sl st in first st.
Round 9: Ch1 (does not count as st throughout), 2hdc in each st to end, join with a sl st in first st. *(24 sts)*
Round 10: Ch1, *1hdc in next st, 2hdc in next st; rep from * to end, join with a sl st in first st. *(36 sts)*
Round 11: Join in either B or C, ch1, 1sc in each st to end, join with a sl st in first st.
Round 12: Ch1, 1sc BLO in each st to end.
Work in a continuous spiral. PM in last st and move up as each round is finished.

Make the tree:

Rounds 13 to 15: 1sc in each st to end. *(36 sts)*
Round 16: *1sc in each of next 7 sts, sc2tog; rep from * to end. *(32 sts)*
Rounds 17 to 19: 1sc in each st to end.
Round 20: *1sc in each of next 6 sts, sc2tog; rep from * to end. *(28 sts)*
Rounds 21 and 22: 1sc in each st to end.
Round 23: *1sc in each of next 5 sts, sc2tog; rep from * to end. *(24 sts)*
Round 24: 1sc in each st to end.
Round 25: *1sc in each of next 4 sts, sc2tog; rep from * to end. *(20 sts)*
Round 26: 1sc in each st to end.
Round 27: *1sc in each of next 3 sts, sc2tog; rep from * to end. *(16 sts)*
Round 28: 1sc in each st to end.
Round 29: *1sc in each of next 2 sts, sc2tog; rep from * to end. *(12 sts)*
Round 30: 1sc in each st to end.
Stuff the tree.
Round 31: *1sc, sc2tog; rep from * to end. *(8 sts)*
Round 32: 1sc in each st to end.
Round 33: [Sc2tog] to end. *(4 sts)*
Round 34: 1sc in each st to end.
Round 35: [Sc2tog] twice. *(2 sts)*
Fasten off.

RUFFLE EDGING
(make one for each tree in matching yarn)
Using US size C/2–D/3 (3mm) hook, ch151.
Starting in 2nd ch from hook, *(1sc, 1hdc) in next ch, (1hdc, 1sc) in next ch, sl st in next ch; rep from * to end.
Fasten off.

LARGE STAR
(make 16)
Round 1: Using A and US size C/2–D/3 (3mm) hook, make a magic ring, 5sc into the ring.
Work in a continuous spiral, do not join.
Round 2: 2sc in each st to end. *(10 sts)*
Round 3: *1sc, 2sc in next st; rep from * to end, join with a sl st in first st. *(15 sts)*
Round 4: *Ch7, sl st in 2nd ch from hook, 1sc in next ch, 1hdc in next ch, 1dc in next ch, 1tr in next ch, miss last ch and next 2 sts of center, sl st in next st of center; rep from * 4 more times around (5 points), ending last point with sl st in base of first point.
Fasten off.

SMALL STAR
(make 7)
Round 1: Using E and US size B/1 (2mm) hook, make a magic ring, 5sc into the ring, join with a sl st in first st.
Round 2: *Ch3, sl st in 2nd ch from hook, 1sc in next ch, sl st in next st of center; rep from * 4 more times around (5 points), ending last point with sl st in base of first point.
Fasten off.

Making up and finishing

Place two of the large stars WS together and use a needle and yarn to oversew together all around the edge.
Using E or F, add French knots (see page 125) along the ruffle edging for each tree. Wind the ruffle all the way around the tree and pin to hold. Stitch in place securely with a needle and thread.
Stitch one small gold star to the top of each tree.
Make a hanging loop in thin string and stitch onto each tree and large star.
Thread the trees and large stars onto the cord and stitch in place with a needle and thread to stop them slipping along the cord.
Add coordinating bows at each end of the garland and stitch in place.

Holly and Birds Wreath

Dark green holly leaves, with their burst of bright red berries, give these golden Christmas birds a perfect bower to nestle in. The birds are worked in yarn that has a metallic thread in it, so they catch the light beautifully against the contrast of the natural twig wreath.

For the wreath

HOLLY LEAF

(make 17)

Using A and US size C/2–D/3 (3mm) hook, ch12.

Round 1: 1sc in 2nd ch from hook, 1sc in next ch, 1hdc in each of next 3 ch, 1dc in each of next 2 ch, 1hdc in each of next 2 ch, 1sc in each of last 2 ch, do not turn, ch1, working back down other side of ch, miss first ch, 1sc in each of first 2 ch, 1hdc in each of next 3 ch, 1dc in each of next 2 ch, 1hdc in each of next 2 ch, 1sc in last ch, ch6, sl st in each ch to base of leaf, sl st in bottom of leaf to join.

Round 2:

Point 1: Sl st in next st of leaf, ch2, sl st in 2nd ch from hook, sl st in next st on leaf.

Point 2: 1sc in next st of leaf, ch2, sl st in 2nd ch from hook, sl st in next st on leaf.

Point 3: 1sc in next st of leaf, ch3, sl st in 3rd ch from hook, sl st in next st on leaf.

Point 4: 1sc in next st of leaf, ch2, sl st in 2nd ch from hook, sl st in next st on leaf.

Point 5: Sl st in next st of leaf, ch2, sl st in 2nd ch from hook, sl st in next st on leaf.

Point 6: Sl st in top st of leaf, ch3, sl st in 2nd ch from hook, sl st in top st of leaf.

Point 7: Rep point 5.

Point 8: Rep point 4.

Point 9: Rep point 3.

SKILL LEVEL ●●●

YARN AND MATERIALS

Rico Baby Cotton Soft (50% cotton, 50% acrylic) light worsted (DK) weight yarn, approx. 136yd (125m) per 1¾oz (50g) ball
- 2 balls of Alga 084 (A)

King Cole Glitz (97% acrylic, 3% polyester) light worsted (DK) weight yarn, approx. 317yd (290m) per 3½oz (100g) ball
- 1 ball each of shades:
- Flame 3504 (B)
- Antique Gold 3503 (C)

Gold embroidery floss

Polyester toy stuffing

Black embroidery floss

11½in (30cm) diameter wicker wreath

Pins

Ribbon for hanging loop and bow

HOOKS AND EQUIPMENT

US size C/2–D/3 (3mm) and US size B/1 (2mm) crochet hooks

Stitch marker

Yarn needle

Hot glue gun

FINISHED MEASUREMENTS

Wreath: 11½in (30cm) diameter

Each holly leaf: 2¾in (7cm)

GAUGE (TENSION)

15 sts x 15 rows = 2¾ x 2½in (7 x 6.5cm) working single crochet, using a US size C/2–D/3 (3mm) hook and Rico Baby Cotton Soft.

15 sts x 15 rows = 2⅜in (6cm) square working single crochet, using a US size C/2–D/3 (3mm) crochet hook and King Cole Glitz.

ABBREVIATIONS

See page 127.

Point 10: Rep point 2.
Point 11: Rep point 1, join with a sl st in base of leaf.
Fasten off.

HOLLY BERRY

(make 16)
Round 1: Using B and US size C/2–D/3 (3mm) hook, make a magic ring, 3sc into the ring.
Work in a continuous spiral, do not join.
Round 2: 2sc in each st to end. *(6 sts)*
Round 3: [Sc2tog] to end.
Fasten off, using long end to gather and close hole.

BIRD

(make 2)
Round 1: Using C and US size C/2–D/3 (3mm) hook, make a magic ring, 6sc into the ring.
Work in a continuous spiral. PM in last st and move up as each round is finished.
Round 2: 2sc in each st to end. *(12 sts)*
Round 3: *1sc, 2sc in next st; rep from * to end. *(18 sts)*
Rounds 4 to 6: 1sc in each st to end.
Round 7: 1sc in each of first 10 sts, 2sc in next st, 1sc in each of next 2 sts, 2sc in next st, 1sc in each of last 4 sts. *(20 sts)*
Round 8: 1sc in each of first 12 sts, [2sc in next st, 1sc in next st] 4 times. *(24 sts)*
Round 9: 1sc in each st to end.
Round 10: 1sc in each of first 15 sts, [2sc in next st, 1sc in each of next 2 sts] 3 times. *(27 sts)*
Round 11: 1sc in each of first 14 sts, 2sc in next st, 1sc in each of next 3 sts, 1hdc in each of next 5 sts, 1sc in each of next 3 sts, 2sc in last st. *(29 sts)*
Round 12: 1sc in each of first 4 sts, sc2tog, 1sc, sc2tog, 1sc in each of next 9 sts, 2sc in next st, 1sc in each of next 2 sts, 2sc in next st, 1sc in each of last 7 sts. *(29 sts)*
Round 13: 1sc in each of first 5 sts, sc2tog, 1sc in each of next 5 sts, 2sc in next st, 1sc in each of next 2 sts, 2sc in next st, 1sc in each of next 3 sts, 1hdc, 1sc in each of next 2 sts, 2sc in next st, 1sc in each of last 6 sts. *(31 sts)*
Round 14: 1sc in each of first 5 sts, [sc2tog] twice, 1sc in each of next 10 sts, 1hdc in each of next 6 sts, 1sc in each of last 6 sts. *(29 sts)*
Round 15: 1sc in each of first 4 sts, [sc2tog] twice, 1sc, sc2tog, 1sc in each of last 18 sts. *(26 sts)*
Round 16: 1sc in each of first 2 sts, [sc2tog] 4 times, 1sc in each of next 5 sts, 1hdc in each of next 8 sts, 1sc in each of last 3 sts. *(22 sts)*
Round 17: 1sc in each of first 3 sts, [sc2tog] twice and stop. Join 2 sides tog along bottom of bird with a sc seam, working 6sc.
Lightly stuff head and bottom curve of body.
Make the tail:
Row 1: Flatten end of bird, ch1, 4sc evenly across tail end, turn.
Row 2: Ch1, 2sc in each st to end, turn. *(8 sts)*
Row 3: Ch1, sl st in first st, miss next 2 sts, (1sc, 1hdc, 1dc, 1tr) in next st, ch2, sl st in 2nd ch from hook, (1tr, 1dc, 1hdc, 1sc) in next st, miss 2 sts, sl st in last st.
Fasten off.

WING 1

(make 2)
Using C and US size C/2–D/3 (3mm) hook, ch7.
Row 1: 1sc in 2nd ch from hook, 1sc in next ch, 1hdc in each of next 2 ch, 1dc in each of next 2 ch (3dc, 1sc) in last ch, do not turn, working back down other side of ch, 1sc in each of next 5 ch, join with a sl st in first st.
Fasten off.

WING 2

(make 2)
Using C and US size C/2–D/3 (3mm) hook, ch7.
Row 1: 1sc in 2nd ch from hook, 1sc in each of next 5ch, do not turn, working back down other side of ch, 4dc in same ch as last sc, 1dc in next ch, 1hdc in each of next 2 ch, 1sc in each of next 2 ch, join with a sl st in first st.
Fasten off.

BEAK

(make 2)
Using gold embroidery floss and US size B/1 (2mm) hook, ch2.
Row 1: 2sc in 2nd ch from hook, turn. *(2 sts)*
Row 2: Ch1, 1sc in first st, 2sc in last st, turn. *(3 sts)*
Row 3: Ch1, 2sc in first st, 1sc, 2sc in last st, turn. *(5 sts)*
Row 4: Ch1, 2sc in first st, 1sc in each of next 3 sts, 2sc in last st. *(7 sts)*
Fasten off, leaving a long tail.

Making up and finishing

Block the leaves.
To finish each bird, sew a wing on each side with the pointed end toward the front. Sew the eyes using black embroidery floss. Use the long end to secure the beak shape, then sew each beak to a bird.
Lay the wreath on a flat surface and use blocking pins to position the leaves, berries, and birds where you want them to be. Glue firmly in place with a hot glue gun.
To finish off the wreath, add a hanging loop and bow at the top of the wreath and stitch or glue in place.

Mistletoe Wreath

This stylish and simple wreath will add a festive feel to any room over the Christmas season—and with the leaves being quick and simple to make, you'll find yourself making them for friends and loved ones, too!

SKILL LEVEL •

YARN AND MATERIALS

James C Brett Twinkle (3% polyester, 97% acrylic) light worsted (DK) weight yarn, 328yd (300m) per 3½oz (100g) ball

1 ball in each of:
Emerald shade TK22 (A)
White shade TK2 (B)

10in (25cm) diameter wicker wreath, sprayed with artificial snow

Ribbon for a hanging loop

HOOKS AND EQUIPMENT

US size C/2–D/3 (3mm) crochet hook

Yarn needle

Hot glue gun

FINISHED MEASUREMENTS

Wreath: 10in (25cm) diameter

Each mistletoe (beg of stem to tip of leaf): 2¾in (7cm)

GAUGE (TENSION)

15 sts x 15 rows = 2¾ x 2½in (7 x 6.5cm) working single crochet, using a US size C/2–D/3 (3mm) crochet hook.

ABBREVIATIONS

See page 127.

Wreath

MISTLETOE

(make 10)

Using A, ch11.

Leaf 1: Sl st in second ch from hook, sl st in each of next 3 ch, 1sc in each of next 4 ch, 1hdc, 2hdc in the last ch, do not turn, working back down other side of ch, 1hdc in each of first 4 ch, 1sc in each of next 3 ch, sl st in each of last 3 ch.

Stalk: Ch12, sl st in second ch from hook, sl st in each of next 10 ch, ending at base of leaf 1.

Leaf 2: Ch11, 1hdc in second ch from hook, 1hdc in each of next 4 ch, 1sc in each of next 3 ch, sl st in each of last 2 ch, do not turn, ch1, working back down other side of ch, miss first ch, sl st in each of next 2 ch, 1sc in each of next 4 ch, 1hdc in each of last 3 ch, sl st in first st to join.

Fasten off.

Making up and finishing

To complete each mistletoe sprig, embroider 2 to 3 French knots (see page 125) in B where the two leaves meet at the bottom. The knots will also serve to hold the leaves together.

Use a hot glue gun to stick the leaves into position. Finish the wreath by adding a hanging loop in coordinating ribbon.

Mistletoe and Hearts Garland

Mistletoe and hearts go hand in hand on this simple Christmas garland—and with tiny white bells used for the mistletoe berries, you can give it a little shake to let someone know you are waiting underneath, ready for your festive kiss!

For the mistletoe leaves

FOR LEAF 1

Work in a continuous spiral, PM at end of round and move up as each round is finished.

Using either a US size G/6 (4mm), a US size C/2-D/3 (3mm) or a US size B/1-C/2 (2.5mm) hook and A, make a magic ring.

Round 1: 4sc into ring. (4 sts)

Round 2: [1sc, 2sc in next st] twice. (6 sts)

Round 3: 1sc, 2sc in next st, 3sc, 2sc in next st. (8 sts)

Round 4: 8sc.

Round 5: 6sc, 2sc in each of next 2 sts. (10 sts)

Rounds 6 and 7: 10sc.

Round 8: 4sc, sc2tog, 4sc. (9 sts)

Round 9: 4sc, sc2tog, 3sc. (8 sts)

Round 10: [2sc, sc2tog] twice. (6 sts)

Rounds 11 to 14: 6sc.

Fasten off, leaving a yarn tail.

FOR LEAF 2

Work in a continuous spiral, PM at end of round and move up as each round is finished.

Using either a US size G/6 (4mm), a US size C/2-D/3 (3mm) or a US size B/1-C/2 (2.5mm) hook and A, make a magic ring.

Round 1: 6sc into ring. (6 sts)

Round 2: [2sc, 2sc in next st] twice. (8 sts)

Round 3: [1sc, 2sc in next st] 4 times. (12 sts)

Round 4: 12sc.

Round 5: 6sc, sc2tog, 4sc. (10 sts)

Rounds 6 and 7: 10sc.

Round 8: 4sc, sc2tog, 4sc. (9 sts)

Round 9: 4sc, sc2tog, 3sc. (8 sts)

Round 10: [2sc, sc2tog] twice. (6 sts)

Rounds 11 to 14: 6sc.

Fasten off, leaving a yarn tail.

For the heart

(make 8 pieces)

Each heart is made up of two pieces.

Using a US size C/2-D/3 (3mm) hook and B, ch2.

Row 1: 2sc in second ch from hook, turn. (2 sts)

Row 2: Ch1 (does not count as a st throughout), 1sc, 2sc in next st, turn. (3 sts)

Row 3: Ch1, 2sc in first st, 1sc, 2sc in last st, turn.

Rows 4 to 6: Ch1, 2sc in first st, 1sc in each st to last st, 2sc in last st. (11 sts at end Row 6)

Row 7: Ch1, 11sc, turn.

Rows 8 to 10: Ch1, 2sc in first st, 1sc in each st to last st, 2sc in last st, turn. (17 sts at end Row 10)

SKILL LEVEL ●●

YARN AND MATERIALS

Cascade Yarns Ultra Pima (100% cotton) light worsted (DK) weight yarn, 219yd (200m) per 3½oz (100g) ball
1 ball of Summer Moss 3780 (A)

Rico Creative Lamé (62% polyester, 38% polyamide) sport (4-ply) weight yarn, 148yd (135m) per ⅞oz (25g) ball
1 ball of Gold 002 (B)

Packet of 14in (35.5cm) 26-gauge floral stem wire

Roll of florist's green stem tape

78in (2m) of ¼in (5mm) ribbon

10 white craft bells (beads or buttons could also be used)

51¼in (130cm) of ¼in (5mm) gold cord

Sewing thread

HOOKS AND EQUIPMENT

US size G/6 (4mm), US size C/2-D/3 (3mm) and US size B/1-C/2 (2.5mm) crochet hooks

Stitch marker

Yarn needle

Sewing needle

FINISHED MEASUREMENTS

Length: Approx. 40in (1m)

GAUGE (TENSION)

Exact gauge (tension) is not essential on this project.

ABBREVIATIONS

See page 127.

NOTE

There are three sprigs of mistletoe on the garland, one six-leafed sprig (three pairs) in the center, and two four-leafed sprigs (two pairs) on each end of the garland. The pattern for each pair of leaves is the same and the different size of each pair of leaves is created by working with different-sized crochet hooks.

For the six-leafed sprig, work three pairs of leaves 1 and 2, using a US size G/6 (4mm) hook, a US size C/2-D/3 (3mm) hook and a US size B/1-C/2 (2.5mm) hook.

For the two smaller sprigs, work two pairs of leaves 1 and 2 using a US size C/2-D/3 (3mm) hook and a US size B/1-C/2 (2.5mm) hook.

Rows 11 and 12: Ch1, 17sc, turn.
Row 13: Ch1, 8sc, turn leaving rem 9 sts unworked. (8 sts)
Row 14: Ch1, sc2tog, 4sc, sc2tog, turn. (6 sts)
Row 15: Sc2tog, 2sc, sc2tog, turn. (4 sts)
Row 16: Sc2tog, 1sc, sl st.
Fasten off and sew in ends.
With completed heart top on left-hand side, join B at right-hand side with a sl st, 1sc in same st, 1sc in each of next 7 sts leaving center st unworked, turn. (8 sts)
Rep Rows 14 to 16.
Fasten off.

Making up and finishing

Bend a stem wire in half loosely, so that you have created a loop at the bent end. Thread this end into one of the leaves, to provide a frame around the inside of the leaf edge. Twist the rest of the wire together to create one stem. Repeat on all the leaves. Use the yarn tail to close up the remaining opening on each leaf, leaving any remaining yarn tail.
Put the leaves into their pairs and use the remaining yarn tail to stitch the two leaves in each pair together at the point where the stem starts. Twist the wires together so that you now have two leaves on one stem. Use florist's tape to cover the stem wires.
Put the pairs of leaves into their sprigs and use a piece of stem wire to bind the stems together.
Cover the wire binding with a short length of ribbon that can then become a hanging loop.
Finish each sprig by adding three bells to each of the medium sprigs and four bells to the large sprigs.
Place two heart pieces together and using B, join them with a single crochet seam. Work a few increases around the curves if needed. Before completely closing each heart, stuff lightly.
Fasten off and sew in ends.
Thread a length of ribbon into the top of each heart for a hanging loop.
Lay the gold cord on a flat surface and tie a knot and loop in each end. Position the mistletoe sprigs and the hearts and thread them on to the cord. Using the sewing needle and thread, add a couple of holding stitches to secure the ribbon to the cord.

Christmas Bauble Wreath

Brightly colored baubles are the perfect decoration to mark the beginning of the festive season—and this wreath allows you to display them anywhere in your home. All the baubles have a touch of glitter and some have added metallic spots.

SKILL LEVEL ●●●

YARN AND MATERIALS

Rico Ricorumi Twinkly Twinkly (99% cotton, 1% polyester) light worsted (DK) weight yarn, approx. 62yd (57m) per ⅞oz (25g) ball

4 balls each of shades:
Red 009 (A)
Green 014 (B)
Rainbow 002 (C)

Anchor Artiste Metallic (80% viscose, 20% polyester) thread, approx. 109yd (100m) per ⅞oz (25g) ball

1 ball of White 304 (D)

6 polystyrene balls, 2in (50mm) diameter

10 polystyrene balls, 1½in (40mm) diameter

12in (30cm) diameter twig wreath

Coordinating ribbon for hanging loop

HOOKS AND EQUIPMENT

US size C/2–D/3 (3mm) crochet hook

Stitch marker

Hot glue gun

FINISHED MEASUREMENTS

Wreath: 12in (30cm) diameter

GAUGE (TENSION)

15 sts x 15 rows = 2¾ x 2½in (7 x 6.5cm) working single crochet, using a US size C/2–D/3 (3mm) crochet hook and Rico Ricorumi Twinkly Twinkly.

ABBREVIATIONS

See page 127.

For the wreath

LARGE BAUBLE

(make 2 in each of A, B, and C)

Round 1: Using either A, B, or C, make a magic ring, 6sc into the ring.

Work in a continuous spiral. PM in last st and move up as each round is finished.

Round 2: 2sc in each st to end. *(12 sts)*

Round 3: *1sc, 2sc in next st; rep from * to end. *(18 sts)*

Round 4: *1sc in each of next 2 sts, 2sc in next st; rep from * to end. *(24 sts)*

Round 5: *1sc in each of next 3 sts, 2sc in next st; rep from * to end. *(30 sts)*

Round 6: *1sc in each of next 4 sts, 2sc in next st; rep from * to end. *(36 sts)*

Rounds 7 to 13: 1sc in each st to end.

Insert 2in (50mm) polystyrene ball.

Round 14: *1sc in each of next 4 sts, sc2tog; rep from * to end. *(30 sts)*

Round 15: *1sc in each of next 3 sts, sc2tog; rep from * to end. *(24 sts)*

Round 16: *1sc in each of next 2 sts, sc2tog; rep from * to end. *(18 sts)*

Rounds 17 and 18: 1sc in each st to end.

Round 19: *1sc, sc2tog; rep from * to end. *(12 sts)*

Round 20: 1sc in each st to end.

Round 21: [Sc2tog] to end.

Fasten off.

MEDIUM BAUBLE

(make 4 in A, 3 in B, 3 in C)

Round 1: Using either A, B or C, make a magic ring, 5sc into the ring.

Round 2: 2sc in each st to end. *(10 sts)*

Round 3: *1sc, 2sc in next st; rep from * to end. *(15 sts)*

Round 4: *1sc in each of next 2 sts, 2sc in next st; rep from * to end. *(20 sts)*

Round 5: *1sc in each of next 3 sts, 2sc in next st; rep from * to end. *(25 sts)*

Round 6: *1sc in each of next 4 sts, 2sc in next st; rep from * to end. *(30 sts)*

Rounds 7 to 11: 1sc in each st to end.

Insert 1½in (40mm) polystyrene ball.

Round 12: *1sc in each of next 4 sts, sc2tog; rep from * to end. *(25 sts)*

Round 13: *1sc in each of next 3 sts, sc2tog; rep from * to end. *(20 sts)*

Rounds 14 and 15: 1sc in each st to end.

Round 16: *1sc in each of next 2 sts, sc2tog; rep from * to end. *(15 sts)*

Round 17: *1sc, sc2tog; rep from * to end. *(10 sts)*

Round 18: [Sc2tog] to end.

Fasten off.

Making up and finishing

Using D, add French knots (see page 125) to one of each of the 2in (50mm) baubles in A, B, and C, and to two of each of the 1½in (40mm) baubles in A, B, and C.

Lay the wreath on a flat surface and use blocking pins to position the baubles where you want them to be. Glue firmly in place with a hot glue gun.

To finish off the wreath, add a coordinating ribbon and hanging loop at the top and stitch or glue in place.

Snowflake Wreath

Delicate snowflakes decorate this charming wreath, each with a touch of glitter to catch the light. It's worked in a neutral color palette and will add a touch of winter glamor to any décor.

For the wreath

LARGE SNOWFLAKE

(make 4 in A, 3 in B, 3 in C)

Round 1: Using A, B, or C, make a magic ring, 6sc into the ring.
Work in a continuous spiral, do not join.

Round 2: 2sc in each st to end, join with a sl st in first st. *(12 sts)*

Round 3: *Ch4, sl st in 2nd ch from hook, ch3, sl st in 3rd ch from hook, ch2, sl st in 2nd ch from hook, sl st in same ch as first sl st of rep, sl st in each of next 2 ch from 4-ch, sl st in center st at base of 4-ch, sl st in next st of center, ch2, sl st in 2nd ch from hook, sl st in center st at base of 2-ch, sl st in next st of center; rep from * 5 more times around center (6 points), ending last point with sl st in base of first point.
Fasten off.

SMALL SNOWFLAKE

(make 3 in A, 4 in B, 4 in C)

Round 1: Using A, B or C, make a magic ring, 6sc into the ring, join with a sl st in first st.

Round 2: *Ch4, sl st in 2nd ch from hook, ch3, sl st in 3rd ch from hook, ch2, sl st in 2nd ch from hook, sl st in same ch as first sl st of rep, sl st in each of next 2 ch from 4-ch, sl st in center st at base of 4-ch, sl st in next st of center; rep from * 5 more times around center (6 points), ending last point with sl st in base of first point.
Fasten off.

Making up and finishing

Block the snowflakes.

Lay the wreath on a flat surface and gently rub on some of the silver rubbing wax. Using blocking pins, position the blocked snowflakes where you want them to be. Glue firmly in place with a hot glue gun. To finish off the wreath, add a coordinating ribbon and hanging loop at the top and stitch or glue in place.

SKILL LEVEL ●●●

YARN AND MATERIALS

King Cole Baby Glitz (97% acrylic, 3% polyester) light worsted (DK) weight yarn, approx. 317yd (290m) per 3½oz (100g) ball

1 ball each of shades:
Silver 3093 (A)
Diamond White 483 (B)
Cream 105 (C)

12in (30cm) diameter twig wreath

Silver rubbing wax

Coordinating ribbon for hanging loop

HOOKS AND EQUIPMENT

US size B/1–C/2 (2.5mm) crochet hook

Hot glue gun

FINISHED MEASUREMENTS

Each large snowflake: 2¼in (5.5cm) from point to opposite point

Each small snowflake: 2in (5cm) from point to opposite point

Wreath: 12in (30cm) diameter

GAUGE (TENSION)

15 sts x 15 rows = 2¾ x 2⅜in (7 x 6cm) working single crochet, using a US size B/1–C/2 (2.5mm) crochet hook.

ABBREVIATIONS

See page 127.

Nordic Wreath

Sometimes the simplest of designs is all that is needed and that's very much the case with this wreath. Just holly leaves and berries, a simple heart, and some red ribbon provide all the Christmassy feel you need!

SKILL LEVEL •

YARN AND MATERIALS

Cascade Yarns Ultra Pima (100% cotton) light worsted (DK) weight yarn, 219yd (200m) per 3½oz (100g) ball

1 ball each of:
Emerald shade 3737 (A)
Lipstick Red shade 3755 (B)
White shade 3728 (C)

Small amount of 100% polyester toy stuffing

1yd (1m) of ⅜in (10mm) wide red gingham ribbon

12in (30cm) twiggy wreath base

Short length of ¼in (5mm) wide red ribbon

10in (25cm) of 1in (25mm) wide red velvet ribbon

HOOKS AND EQUIPMENT

US size B/1–C/2 (2.5mm) crochet hook

Yarn needle

Hot glue gun

FINISHED MEASUREMENTS

12in (30cm) diameter

GAUGE (TENSION)

One holly leaf measures approx. 2½in (6.5cm) long, using US size B/1–C/2 (2.5mm) crochet hook and Cascade Yarns Ultra Pima.

ABBREVIATIONS

See page 127.

SPECIAL ABBREVIATIONS

MP (make picot): ch2, sl st in second ch from hook.

Holly berries

(make 17)

Using US size B/1–C/2 (2.5mm) hook and B, make a magic ring.

Round 1: 4sc in ring. *(4 sts)*

Round 2: [1sc in next st, 2sc in next st] twice, sl st in first sc to join. *(6 sts)*

Fasten off, leaving a long yarn tail.

Use the yarn tail to close each holly berry at the back by running a gathering thread around the base and pulling it up tightly.

Holly leaves

(make 14)

Using US size B/1–C/2 (2.5mm) hook and A, ch12.

Round 1: 1sc in second ch from hook, 1sc in each of next 2 ch, 1hdc in each of next 2 ch, 1dc in each of next 2 ch, 1hdc in each of next 2 ch, 1sc in next ch, (1sc, ch1, 1sc in last ch, working down opposite side of ch, 1sc in each of next 2 ch, 1hdc in each of next 2 ch, 1dc in each of next 2 ch, 1hdc in each of next 2 ch, 1sc in each of next 2 ch, sl st in first st to join.

Round 2: [(1sc, MP, 1sc) in next st, sl st in next st] 5 times, (sl st, ch3, sl st in third ch from hook, sl st) in next st, working down opposite side of leaf, [(1sc, MP, 1sc) in next st, sl st in next st] 5 times, MP, sl st in first st to join.

Fasten off.

Heart

(make 2)

Using US size B/1–C/2 (2.5mm) hook and B, ch2.

Row 1: 2sc in second ch from hook. *(2 sts)*

Turn at end of this and every foll row.

Row 2: Ch1, 1sc in first st, 2sc in next st. *(3 sts)*

Row 3: Ch1, 2sc in first st, 1sc in next st, 2sc in next st. *(5 sts)*

Rows 4–6: Ch1, 2sc in first st, 1sc in each st to last st, 2sc in last st. *(11 sts)*

Row 7: Ch1, 1sc in each st to end.

Rows 8–10: Ch1, 2sc in first st, 1sc in each st to last st, 2sc in last st. *(17 sts)*

Rows 11–12: Ch1, 1sc in each st to end.

LOBE

Row 13: Ch1, 1sc in each of first 8 sts, turn.

Row 14: Ch1, 1sc in each of next 8 sts, turn.

Row 15: Sc2tog, 1sc in each of next 4 sts, sc2tog, turn. *(6 sts)*

Row 16: Ch1, sc2tog, 1sc in each of next 2 sts, sc2tog, turn. *(4 sts)*

Row 17: Ch1, [sc2tog] twice. *(2 sts)*

Fasten off.

Rejoin yarn at other end of Row 13 and rep Rows 13–17 for second lobe.

Using B, work sc evenly around edge of heart, working a couple of extra sc around lobes to keep shape if needed.

Fasten off.

Making up and finishing

Sew in ends of all pieces. Tie one end of the ⅜in (10mm) gingham ribbon to the back of the wreath base and wrap the ribbon all the way around the wreath following the photograph as a guide, so that you have seven spaces in total between each ribbon wrap. Tie the ribbon securely at the back to finish.

Using the hot glue gun, stick two holly leaves and two or three berries into each space on the wreath.

Using a yarn needle threaded with C, embroider a simple Nordic design onto one of the heart pieces, following the photo as a guide. Using a yarn needle threaded with C, place the two hearts WS together and join by sewing blanket stitch all the way around the edge. Before finishing the seam, stuff slightly, then close the heart and fasten off. Sew in any ends. Thread the ¼in (5mm) red ribbon through the top of the heart and tie it to the wreath at the center top.

Use the velvet ribbon to make a hanging loop at the back of the wreath.

Christmas Stocking String

This garland works brilliantly as an alternative Advent calendar, because both the stockings and the buckets can have little treats tucked away inside them. Once made, this garland can be brought out every year with the rest of your favorite festive decorations.

Stocking

(make 2 in A and B, 2 in A and C)

Using US size E/4 (3.5mm) hook and A, make a magic ring.

Round 1: 6sc in ring. *(6 sts)*

Work in a continuous spiral. PM in last st and move up as each round is finished.

Round 2: 2sc in each st to end. *(12 sts)*

Round 3: [1sc in next st, 2sc in next st] 6 times. *(18 sts)*

Rounds 4–11: 1sc in each st to end.

Round 12: 1sc in each st to end, working last yoh in either B or C.

Row 13: Using B or C, 1sc in each of first 12 sts, turn.

Rows 14–16: Ch1 (does not count as st), 1sc in each of next 12 sts, turn. *(12 sts)*

Fold foot flat, with second color panel at heel. Working so seam will be on inside of stocking, join back of heel with a sc seam across the first 5 sts (working into corresponding sts from both sides of heel), work a sl st to join final pair of heel sts, completing the heel seam.

Fasten off B or C.

Round 17: Using A, work 15 sc evenly around opening of foot. *(15 sts)*

Round 18: Work 1sc in each st to end, working 2sc in each of 2 center back sts above heel seam. *(17 sts)*

Rounds 19–25: 1sc in each st to end.

Round 26: 1sc in each st to end, working last yoh in either B or C.

Fasten off A.

Rounds 27–28: Using B or C, 1sc in each st to end.

Round 29: 2sc in first st, 1sc in each of next 9 sts, 2sc in next st, 1sc in each of next 6 sts. *(19 sts)*

Rounds 30 and 31: 1sc in each st to end, sl st in top of first sc to join at end of last round.

Fasten off.

SKILL LEVEL ••

YARN AND MATERIALS

Cascade Yarns Ultra Pima (100% cotton) light worsted (DK) weight yarn, 219yd (200m) per 3½oz (100g) ball

1 ball each of:
- Lipstick Red shade 3755 (A)
- Light Gray shade 3808 (B)
- White shade 3728 (C)

Yarn and Colors Must-Have Minis (100% cotton) fingering (4-ply) weight yarn, 27yd (25m) per ⅓oz (10g) ball

1 ball of White shade 001 (D)

Florist's wire for bucket handles

Card to line buckets

Approx. 1yd (1m) of ⅜in (10mm) wide red gingham ribbon

47in (120cm) of white cord

HOOKS AND EQUIPMENT

US size E/4 (3.5mm) crochet hook

US size B/1–C/2 (2.5mm) crochet hook

Locking stitch marker

Yarn needle

Sewing needle and thread

FINISHED MEASUREMENTS

Garland: length 35½in (90cm)

Bucket: height 2in (5cm), top diameter 2¼in (5.5cm)

Stocking: approx. length 4in (10cm)

GAUGE (TENSION)

15 sts x 15 rows = 2½ x 3in (6.5 x 7.5cm) working single crochet, using a US size E/4 (3.5mm) crochet hook and Cascade Yarns Ultra Pima.

ABBREVIATIONS

See page 127.

Bucket

(make 3)

BASE

Using US size E/4 (3.5mm) hook and B, make a magic ring.

Round 1: 6sc in ring. *(6 sts)*

Work in a continuous spiral. PM in last st and move up as each round is finished.

Round 2: 2sc in each st to end. *(12 sts)*

Round 3: [1sc in next st, 2sc in next st] 6 times. *(18 sts)*

Round 4: 1sc in next st, 2sc in next st, [1sc in each of next 2 sts, 2sc in next st] 5 times, 1sc in last st. *(24 sts)*

Round 5: [1sc in each of next 3 sts, 2sc in next st] 6 times, sl st in top of first sc to join round. *(30 sts)*

SIDES

Beg working in rounds.

Round 6: Ch1 (does not count as st throughout), working in back loop only of each st, 1sc in each st to end, sl st in top of ch-1 to join. *(30 sts)*

Round 7: Ch1, working in both loops, 1sc in next sc, 1sc in each st to end, sl st in top of ch-1 to join.

Round 8: Ch1, 1sc in each of next 14 sc, 2sc in next st, 1sc in each of next 14 sts, 2sc in next st, sl st in top of ch-1 to join. *(32 sts)*

Rounds 9 and 10: Ch1, 1sc in next sc, 1sc in each st to end, sl st in top of ch-1 to join. *(32 sts)*

Round 11: Ch1, 1sc in each of next 7 sc, 2sc in next st, 1sc in each of next 15 sts, 2sc in next st, 1sc in each of next 8 sts, sl st in top of ch-1 to join. *(34 sts)*

Rounds 12–14: Ch1, 1sc in next sc, 1sc in each st to end, sl st in top of ch-1 to join.

Round 15: Ch1, 1sc in each of next 2 sc, 2sc in next st, 1sc in each of next 16 sts, 2sc in next st, 1sc in each of next 14 sts, sl st in top of ch-1 to join. *(36 sts)*

Rounds 16–17: Ch1, 1sc in next sc, 1sc in each st to end, sl st in top of ch-1 to join.

Round 18: Ch1, sl st loosely in each st to end, sl st in top of ch-1 to join.

Fasten off.

Star

(make 3)

Using US size B/1–C/2 (2.5mm) hook and D, make a magic ring.

Round 1: 5sc in ring. *(5 sts)*

Round 2: [2sc in next st] 5 times, sl st in top of first sc to join. *(10 sts)*

Round 3: *Ch4, sl st in second ch from hook, 1sc in next ch, 1hdc in next ch, miss next st of central circle, sl st in next st of central circle; rep from * 4 times to make 5 points in total, sl st in base of first point to join.

Fasten off.

Making up and finishing

Sew in all ends.

Using a needle and thread sew a star onto each bucket. Make a wire handle for each bucket and stitch each side in place. Line the bucket with card to give the sides rigidity. Cut 3 short lengths of gingham ribbon and tie in a bow around center top of each handle.

Using a yarn needle threaded with D, decorate each stocking with straight stitches and French knots (see page 125), following the photograph as a guide. Fold down the top of the stocking and secure with a couple of small stitches. Cut 4 short lengths of gingham ribbon and stitch a small ribbon loop into the center back of each stocking.

Lay the white cord out on a table and hang the stockings and buckets where you want them to be. Add a couple of stitches with the needle and thread to hold each item in place.

Tie loop knots at each end of the cord and add a bow of gingham ribbon at each end.

TIP

Instead of making the stockings and buckets for the hanging string, why not make the items individually as little place settings for the Christmas table?

Winter Hanging Wreath

Hung above a dinner table, this wreath—with its glass tealight holders—will throw a warm glow over everything below. This is such a simple thing to make, yet it has maximum visual effect.

SKILL LEVEL ●

YARN AND MATERIALS

Cascade Yarns Ultra Pima (100% cotton) light worsted (DK) weight yarn, 219yd (200m) per 3½oz (100g) ball

1 ball in each of:
Summer Moss 3780 (A)
Sage 3720 (B)

Cascade Yarns Heritage (75% merino wool, 25% nylon) sport (4-ply) weight yarn, 437yd (400m) per 3½oz (100g) ball

1 ball in Christmas Red 5619 (C)

12in (30cm) wreath base

4 lengths of ⅜in (10mm) wide ribbon, each 27½in (70cm) long

4 lengths of ¼in (6mm) wide ribbon, each 19¾in (50cm)

Sewing thread

4 hanging glass tealight holders

4 LED tealights

HOOKS AND EQUIPMENT

US size C/2–D/3 (3mm) and US size B/1–C/2 (2.5mm) crochet hooks

Stitch marker

Yarn needle

Blocking pins

Spray starch

Hot glue gun

Sewing needle

FINISHED MEASUREMENTS

Wreath diameter: 12in (30cm)

Large ivy leaf: 2¾ x 2¾in (7 x 7cm)

Small ivy leaf: 2 x 2in (5 x 5cm)

GAUGE (TENSION)

Exact gauge (tension) is not essential on this project.

ABBREVIATIONS

See page 127.

For the large ivy leaves

(make 15)

Work in a continuous spiral for Rounds 1 to 3, PM at end of round and move up as each round is finished.

Using a US size C/2–D/3 (3mm) hook and A, make a magic ring.

Round 1: 6sc into ring. *(6 sts)*

Round 2: [2sc in each st] 6 times. *(12 sts)*

Round 3: [1sc, 2sc in each st] 6 times, sl st in beg st to join. *(18 sts)*

Round 4:

Leaf point 1: Ch4, 1sc in second ch from hook, 2hdc, skip next 2 sts from Round 3, sl st in next st.

Leaf point 2: Ch5, 1sc in second ch from hook, 1hdc, 2dc, skip next 2 sts from Round 3, sl st in next st.

Leaf point 3: Ch7, 1sc in second ch from hook, 1hdc, 1dc, 2tr, 1ttr, skip next 4 sts from Round 3, sl st in next st.

Leaf point 4: Ch5, 1sc in second ch from hook, 1hdc in next st, 2dc, skip next 2 sts from Round 3, sl st in next st.

Leaf point 5: Ch4, 1sc in second ch from hook, 2hdc, skip next st from Round 3, sl st in next st, sl st in beg st to join.

Fasten off A and sew in ends.

EDGING AND STALK

Using a US size B/1–C/2 (2.5mm) hook, join B at the base of Leaf point 1.

Work sc around edge of each leaf. At tip of Leaf points 1, 2, 4 and 5, ch2 and sl st back in first ch. At tip of Leaf point 3, ch3 and sl st back in first ch.

At center base of leaf, ch7 for stalk, starting in second ch from hook, sl st back to base of leaf, sl st in beg st to join.

Fasten off and sew in ends.

For the small ivy leaves

(make 20)

Using a US size C/2–D/3 (3mm) hook and A, make a magic ring.

Round 1: 6sc into ring. *(6 sts)*

Round 2: [2sc in each st] 6 times. *(12 sts)*

Round 3:

Leaf point 1: Ch3, 1sc in second ch from hook, 1hdc, skip next st from Round 2, sl st in next st.

Leaf point 2: Ch4, 1sc in second ch from hook, 2hdc, skip next st from Round 2, sl st in next st.

Leaf point 3: Ch6, 1sc in second ch from hook, 1hdc, 1dc, 2tr, skip next 2 sts from Round 2, sl st in next st.

Leaf point 4: Ch4, 1sc in second ch from hook, 2hdc, skip next st from Round 2, sl st in next st.

Leaf point 5: Ch3, 1sc in second ch from hook, 1hdc, skip next st from Round 2, sl st in next st, sl st in beg st to join.

EDGING AND STALK

Using a US size B/1–C/2 (2.5mm) hook, join B at the base of Leaf point 1.

Work sc around edge of each leaf. At tip of Leaf points 1, 2, 4 and 5, ch2 and sl st back in first ch. At tip of Leaf point 3, ch3 and sl st back in first ch.

At center base of leaf, ch6 for stalk, starting in second ch from hook, sl st back to base of leaf, sl st in beg st to join.

Fasten off and sew in ends.

For the holly leaves

(make 8)

Using a US size C/2–D/3 (3mm) hook and A, ch10.

Round 1: 1sc in second ch from hook, 1hdc, 2dc, 2tr, 2dc, (1hdc, 2 sc) in next st, working down opposite side of ch, 1hdc, 2dc, 1tr, 2dc, 1hdc, 1sc.

STALK

Ch4, starting in second ch from hook, sl st back to base of leaf, sl st in beg st to join.

Round 2:

Point 1: Ch2, sl st in second ch from hook, sl st in next st.

Point 2: Ch3, sl st in second ch from hook, 1sc, skip next 2 sts from Round 1, sl st in next st.

Point 3: Ch3, sl st in second ch from hook, 1sc, skip next 2 sts from Round 1, sl st in next st.

Point 4: Ch3, sl st in second ch from hook, 1sc, skip next 2 sts from Round 1, sl st in next st, 1sc.

Leaf tip: Ch3, sl st in second ch from hook, 1sc, sl st in next st, skip next st from Round 1, sl st in next st.

Point 5: Ch2, sl st in second ch from hook, sl st in next st.

Point 6: Ch3, sl st in second ch from hook, skip next 2 sts from Round 1, sl st in next st.

Point 7: Ch3, sl st in second ch from hook, 1sc, skip next st from Round 1, sl st in next st.
Point 8: Ch2, sl st in second ch from hook, skip next st from Round 1, sl st in base of leaf.
Fasten off and sew in ends.

For the holly berries

(make 12)
Work in a continuous spiral for Rounds 1 to 3, PM at end of round and move up as each round is finished.
Using a US size B/1–C/2 (2.5mm) hook and C, make a magic ring.
Round 1: 5sc into ring. *(5 sts)*
Round 2: [2sc in next st] 5 times. *(10 sts)*
Round 3: 10sc.
Round 4: [Sc2tog] 5 times. *(5 sts)*
Stuff with yarn ends and close up ring, fasten off, and sew in ends.

Making up and finishing

Block all the leaves and leave to air dry.
Lay the wreath on a flat surface and tie the four 27½in (70cm) lengths of ribbon equally around the top of the ring to create the hanging loop. Tie the ribbons in a knot at the top.
Using the hot glue gun, attach the leaves to the wreath base, sticking them mostly around the outside side edge, with a few on the inside sides.
Using a needle and thread, sew two holly leaves across the top of each glass tealight holder. Use the glue gun to stick three berries to each pair of leaves.
Tie a length of 19¾in (50cm) ribbon to each glass holder and then tie each holder to the underside of the wreath securely. You may find this easier to do with the wreath hanging. Place an LED tealight in each of the glass holders—do not use real tealight candles in this wreath.

Mini Christmas Trees

Perfect for lining up on a fireplace or for embellishing a festive table, these little Christmas trees won't need any decorating nor will they shed needles anywhere! Worked in a continuous round, from bottom to top, and with a sparkly spiral for their decoration, each tree measures just 7in (18cm) tall and sits inside its own tin bucket.

For the tree

Work in a continuous spiral starting from center of tree base, PM at end of round, and move up as each round is finished.

Using a US size E/4 (3.5mm) hook and 1 strand each of A and B, make a magic ring.

Round 1: 6sc into ring. *(6 sts)*
Round 2: [2sc in next st] 6 times. *(12 sts)*
Round 3: [1sc, 2sc in next st] 6 times. *(18 sts)*
Round 4: [2sc, 2sc in next st] 6 times. *(24 sts)*
Round 5: [3sc, 2sc in next st] 6 times. *(30 sts)*
Round 6: [4sc, 2sc in next st] 6 times. *(36 sts)*
Round 7: [5sc, 2sc in next st] 6 times. *(42 sts)*
Round 8: [6sc, 2sc in next st] 6 times. *(48 sts)*
Round 9: [7sc, 2sc in next st] 6 times. *(54 sts)*
Round 10: 54sc.
Round 11: 54scBLO.

Draw round base on to card and cut out, place disc of card inside base of tree.

Begin dec for tree top.

Round 12: [7scBLO, sc2tog] 6 times. *(48 sts)*
Rounds 13 to 16: 48scBLO.
Round 17: [6scBLO, sc2tog] 6 times. *(42 sts)*
Rounds 18 to 20: 42scBLO.
Round 21: [5scBLO, sc2tog] 6 times. *(36 sts)*
Rounds 22 to 24: 36scBLO.

SKILL LEVEL ●●

YARN AND MATERIALS

Cascade Yarns Heritage (75% merino wool, 25% nylon) sport (4-ply) weight yarn, 437yd (400m) per 3½oz (100g) ball
- 1 ball in each of:
  - Herb 5658 (A)
  - Moss 5612 (B)

Anchor Artiste Metallic (80% viscose, 20% polyester) thread, 109yd (100m) per ⅞oz (25g) ball
- 1 ball in each of:
  - White 304 (C)
  - Green 322 (D)

Approx. 4 x 4in (10 x 10cm) of thin card (cardstock) per tree

Toy stuffing

Sewing thread

2¼ x 2in (5.5 x 5cm) tin bucket per tree

10in (25cm) of ⅝in (15mm) wide ribbon per tree, in a co-ordinating color

HOOKS AND EQUIPMENT

US size E/4 (3.5mm) and US size steel 4-B/1 (2mm) crochet hooks

Stitch marker

Yarn needle

Sewing needle

Hot glue gun

FINISHED MEASUREMENTS

Height: 7in (18cm)

Width at base: 3¼in (8cm)

Star: 1⅜in (3.5cm)

GAUGE (TENSION)

20 sts x 28 rows = 4 x 4in (10 x 10cm) working single crochet, using a US size E/4 (3.5mm) hook and 2 strands of Cascade Yarns Heritage Superwash.

ABBREVIATIONS

See page 127.

Round 25: [4scBLO, sc2tog] 6 times. *(30 sts)*
Rounds 26 and 27: 30scBLO.
Round 28: [3scBLO, sc2tog] 6 times. *(24 sts)*
Rounds 29 and 30: 24scBLO.
Round 31: [2scBLO, sc2tog] 6 times. *(18 sts)*
Round 32: 18scBLO.
Stuff the tree.
Round 33: [1scBLO, sc2tog] 6 times. *(12 sts)*
Round 34: 12scBLO.
Finish stuffing.
Round 35: [Sc2tog] 6 times.
Fasten off and sew in ends.

TREE DECORATION

Worked in front loop ridges that wind down from top of tree to base.
Using a US size steel 4-B/1 (2mm) hook and either C or D, starting at top of tree, (1sc, ch1) in front loop ridge of each st of first round.
Miss next front loop ridge and drop down to ridge below, (1sc, ch1) in each st.
Keep working this pattern to base of tree.
Fasten off and sew in ends.

For the star

(make 2 for each star, front and back)
Using a US size steel 4-B/1 (2mm) hook and either C or D, make a magic ring.
Round 1: 5sc into ring. *(5 sts)*
Round 2: [2sc in each st] 5 times, sl st in beg st to join. *(10 sts)*
Round 3: *Ch5, sl st in second ch from hook, 1sc, 1hdc, 1dc, miss 1 st from Round 2, sl st next st; rep from * 4 more times (5 points) working the last st st in beg st to join.
Fasten off and sew in ends.

TIP

By working in the alternate front loop ridges for the tree decoration, you are still able to see the tree underneath.

Making up and finishing

Take the two matching stars and place them WS together, stitch all around the edge to join. Sew the star to the top of the tree.
Using a hot glue gun, put glue all around the top edge of the bucket. Position the tree centrally and stick it to the top of the bucket.
Make a bow from the ribbon and stick or sew the bow to the center front of the base of the tree.

Gingerbread Garland

You may not get the delicious smell of warm gingerbread cooking whilst making this garland, but these little gingerbread men and candy canes will last and last and can be brought out every year to decorate your home for the holidays.

SKILL LEVEL ●●●

YARN AND MATERIALS

Schachenmayr Catania (100% cotton) sport (5-ply) weight yarn, approx. 137yd (125m) per 1¾oz (50g) ball
1 ball each of shades:
Sun-Kissed shade 437 (brown) (A)
Strawberry shade 258 (red) (B)

10 toy safety eyes, ⅛in (3mm) size

Polyester toy stuffing

4 pipe cleaners, 12in (30cm) long

4 green buttons, ⅛in (3mm) diameter

6 red buttons, ⅛in (3mm) diameter

5 small red ribbon bows

Red embroidery floss

Thin string for hanging loops

60in (150cm) gold cord

4 short lengths of narrow green velvet ribbon

2 lengths of wide green velvet ribbon

HOOKS AND EQUIPMENT

US size B/1–C/2 (2.5mm) crochet hook

Stitch marker

Needle and matching thread

Pins

FINISHED MEASUREMENTS

Each gingerbread man: 3¼in (8cm) tall

Each candy cane: 2¾in (7cm) long, with top turned over

Garland: approx. 41½in (105cm) long

GAUGE (TENSION)

15 sts x 15 rows = 2½in (6.5cm) square working single crochet, using a US size B/1–C/2 (2.5mm) crochet hook.

ABBREVIATIONS

See page 127.

For the garland

GINGERBREAD MEN

(make 5)

Round 1: Using A, make a magic ring, 6sc into the ring.
Work in a continuous spiral. PM in last st and move up as each round is finished.
Round 2: 2sc in each st to end. *(12 sts)*
Round 3: *1sc, 2sc in next st; rep from * to end. *(18 sts)*
Round 4: *1sc in each of next 2 sts, 2sc in next st; rep from * to end. *(24 sts)*
Rounds 5 to 7: 1sc in each st to end.
Attach safety eyes, approx. 3 sts apart.
Round 8: *1sc in each of next 2 sts, sc2tog; rep from * to end. *(18 sts)*
Round 9: *1sc in next st, sc2tog; rep from * to end. *(12 sts)*
Round 10: *1sc in next st, sc2tog; rep from * to end. *(8 sts)*
Round 11: 2sc in each of next 7 sts, 1sc in last st. *(15 sts)*
Round 12: *1sc in each of next 2 sts, 2sc in next st; rep from * to end. *(20 sts)*
Rounds 13 to 22: 1sc in each st to end.
Fasten off.
Make the legs:
Lay gingerbread man flat, re-join A to center of front body, and join two bottom edges in center by working 1sc from front to back working through both edges, dividing the bottom opening into two equal leg openings.
Stuff body very lightly.
First leg round 23: 9sc around one leg opening.
Work in a continuous spiral. PM in last st and move up as each round is finished.
First leg rounds 24 to 27: 1sc in each st to end. *(9 sts)*
Stuff leg very lightly.
Round 28: [Sc2tog] to end.
Fasten off.
Second leg: Work as first leg.

ARMS

(make 2 for each man)

Round 1: Using A, make a magic ring, 4sc into the ring.
Work in a continuous spiral. PM in last st and move up as each round is finished.
Round 2: 2sc in each st to end. *(8 sts)*
Rounds 3 to 10: 1sc in each st to end.
Fasten off.

CANDY CANE

(make 4)

Round 1: Using A, make a magic ring, 4sc into the ring.

Work in a continuous spiral. PM in last st and move up as each round is finished.

Round 2: 2sc in each st to end. *(8 sts)*

Rounds 3 to 25: 1sc in each st to end.

Fold a pipe cleaner into three and carefully push inside cane.

Round 26: [Sc2tog] to end.

Fasten off.

CANDY CANE STRIPE

(make 4)

Using B, ch80.

Fasten off.

Making up and finishing

Sew the arms and buttons onto each gingerbread men. Stitch on small red bows for bow ties. Using red embroidery floss, stitch on the mouth.

Turn over the top part of the candy cane to make the hook shape and then wind the stripe all the way around it, pinning in place to hold. Use a needle and thread to stitch into place securely.

Cut short lengths of thin string, thread one through the top of each gingerbread man and cane, and knot to make a hanging loop. Thread the gingerbread men and candy canes onto the cord and stitch in place with a needle and thread to stop them slipping along the cord. Tie the narrow green velvet ribbons into bows and sew one above each candy cane.

Add coordinating bows in wider ribbon at each end of the garland and stitch in place.

Dried Fruit Wreath

With its little bunch of cinnamon sticks and the tiny slices of dried apple and orange, you can almost smell the scent of Christmas coming from this wreath. The sprigs of eucalyptus are wired onto florist's wire, which helps to give the wreath depth and contrast.

For the small eucalyptus leaves

(make 14)

Using a US size E/4 (3.5mm) hook and 1 strand each of A and B held together, make a magic ring.

Round 1: 5sc into ring. *(5 sts)*

Pull up closing yarn tail to form a semi-circle, sl st into ring.

Round 2: (Sl st, 1sc) in first st, (1sc, 1hdc) in next st, 2dc in next st, (1hdc, 1sc) in next st, sl st in next st.

Close ring, fasten off, and sew in ends.

For the medium eucalyptus leaves

(make 14)

Using a US size E/4 (3.5mm) hook and 1 strand each of A and B held together, make a magic ring.

Round 1: 6sc into ring. *(6 sts)*

Pull up closing yarn tail to form a semi-circle, sl st into ring.

Round 2: (1sc, 1hdc) in first st, (1hdc, 1dc) in next st, (1dc, 1tr) in next st, (1tr, 1dc) in next st, (1dc, 1hdc) in next st, (1hdc, 1sc) in next st, sl st in beg sc to join.

Close ring, fasten off, and sew in ends.

For the large eucalyptus leaves

(make 14)

Using a US size E/4 (3.5mm) hook and 1 strand each of A and B held together, make a magic ring.

Round 1: 7sc into ring. *(7 sts)*

SKILL LEVEL ●●

YARN AND MATERIALS

Cascade Yarns Heritage (75% merino wool, 25% nylon) sport (4-ply) weight yarn, 437yd (400m) per 3½oz (100g) ball

1 ball in each of:
- Herb 5658 (A)
- Moss 5612 (B)
- Snow 5618 (C)
- Golden Yellow 5752 (D)
- Cinnamon 5640 (E)
- Wine 5663 (F)

Packet of 14in (35.5cm) 26-gauge floral stem wire

8in (20cm) wreath base

4 cinnamon sticks, each 3⅛in (8cm) long

Small amount of ribbon for tying cinnamon bundle and hanging loop

HOOKS AND EQUIPMENT

US size E/4 (3.5mm) and US size C/2–D/3 (3mm) crochet hooks

Stitch marker

Yarn needle

Blocking pins

Spray starch

Hot glue gun

FINISHED MEASUREMENTS

Wreath diameter: 8in (20cm)

Eucalyptus sprigs: approx. 3⅛in (8cm) long

Orange/apple slices: 1½in (4cm)

GAUGE (TENSION)

Exact gauge (tension) is not essential on this project.

ABBREVIATIONS

See page 127.

NOTE

Each eucalyptus sprig is made up of two small leaves, two medium leaves, and two large leaves. Each leaf is worked with two strands of yarn.

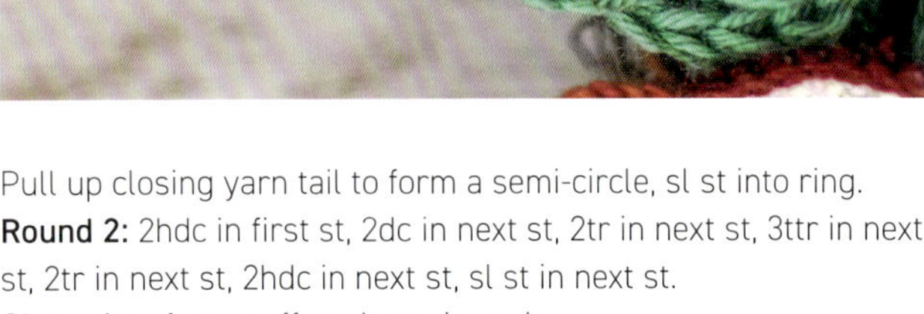

Pull up closing yarn tail to form a semi-circle, sl st into ring.
Round 2: 2hdc in first st, 2dc in next st, 2tr in next st, 3ttr in next st, 2tr in next st, 2hdc in next st, sl st in next st.
Close ring, fasten off, and sew in ends.

For the orange slices

(make 6)
Using a US size C/2-D/3 (3mm) hook and C, make a magic ring.
Round 1: 8sc into ring, sl st into first st to join. *(8 sts)*
Fasten off C.
Now work in a continuous spiral, PM at end of each round and move up as each round is finished.
Round 2: Join D, [2sc in next st] 8 times. *(16 sts)*
Round 3: [1sc, 2sc in next st] 8 times. *(24 sts)*
Round 4: [2sc, 2sc in next st] 8 times. *(32 sts)*
Fasten off D.
Round 5: Join C, 32sc.
Fasten off C.
Round 6: Join E, [3sc, 2sc in next st] 8 times. *(40 sts)*
Fasten off and sew in ends.
Thread a yarn needle with C and embroider six lines for segments between center C round and outer C round.

For the apple slices

(make 6)
Using a US size C/2-D/3 (3mm) hook and C only, work as for orange slices for Rounds 1 to 5.
Fasten off C.
Round 6: Join F, [3sc, 2sc in next st] 8 times. *(40 sts)*
Fasten off and sew in ends.
Thread a yarn needle with F and embroider five pips around center of apple slice.

Making up and finishing

Block all the leaves and fruit slices and leave to air dry.
Bend a stem wire in half and thread a small leaf onto each of the two wire halves, taking the leaves right up to the fold in the wire. Twist the two wires below the two leaves. Thread on the two medium leaves in the same way and twist the wire underneath the leaves. Thread on the two large leaves in the same way. Twist the two wires together below the large leaves to make one stem. Trim the wire to leave a stalk of approx. 1½in (4cm).
Lay the wreath base onto a flat surface and thread the eucalyptus wire stems into it so that they are spread around equally. If needed, secure with glue from the hot glue gun.
Position the apple and orange slices and stick in to place with the hot glue gun.
Tie the cinnamon sticks into a bundle and secure with a piece of ribbon. Stick to the wreath base.
Add a ribbon hanging loop at the center top of the wreath.

CHAPTER 2

For The Home

Holly Pillow

With its simple wreath of leaves in shades of green, vivid red holly berries, and bright pompom edging, this pillow will certainly give a festive feel to any sofa or armchair. It adds a lovely pop of Christmassy color.

Pillow cover front

(make 1)

Using US size H/8 (5mm) hook and A, ch71.

Row 1: 1sc in second ch from hook, 1sc in each ch to end, turn. *(70 sts)*

Row 2: Ch1 (does not count as st), 1sc in each st to end, turn.

Rep Row 2 until work measures 16in (40cm).

BORDER

Round 1: Work a second sc in last st of prev row (corner made), work 1sc in each row end down left-hand side, 2sc in corner st, work 1sc in each st along bottom edge, 2sc in corner st, work 1sc in each row end up right-hand side, 2sc in corner st, sl st in first st of last row of pillow to join.

Fasten off.

Pillow cover upper back

(make 1)

Using US size H/8 (5mm) hook and A, ch71.

Row 1: 1sc in second ch from hook, 1sc in each ch to end, turn. *(70 sts)*

Row 2: Ch1 (does not count as st), 1sc in each st to end, turn.

Rep Row 2 until work measures 10in (25cm).

SKILL LEVEL ●●

YARN AND MATERIALS

Drops Big Merino (100% merino wool) worsted (Aran) weight yarn, 82yd (75m) per 1¾oz (50g) ball

- 9 balls of Beige shade 19 (A)

Cascade Yarns Ultra Pima (100% cotton) light worsted (DK) weight yarn, 219yd (200m) per 3½oz (100g) ball

- 1 ball each of:
  - Sage shade 3720 (B)
  - Emerald shade 3737 (C)

Yarn and Colors Must-Have Minis (100% cotton) fingering (4-ply) weight yarn, 27yd (25m) per ⅓oz (10g) ball

- 1 ball each of:
  - Cardinal shade 031 (D)
  - White shade 001 (E)

16 x 16in (40 x 40cm) pillow pad

2yd (2m) of red pompom edging

Approx. 10in (25cm) of ⅝in (16mm) wide red velvet ribbon

3 buttons

3 snap fasteners

HOOKS AND EQUIPMENT

US size H/8 (5mm) crochet hook

US size E/4 (3.5mm) crochet hook

US size B/1–C/2 (2.5mm) crochet hook

Yarn needle

Safety pins

Sewing needle and thread

Piece of cardboard same size as pillow pad

FINISHED MEASUREMENTS

16½in (42cm) square

GAUGE (TENSION)

15 sts x 15 rows = 3½ x 3in (9 x 7.5cm) working single crochet, using a US size H/8 (5mm) crochet hook and Drops Big Merino.

One holly leaf measures approx. 2¾in (7cm) long, using a US size E/4 (3.5mm) crochet hook and Cascade Yarns Ultra Pima.

ABBREVIATIONS

See page 127.

SPECIAL ABBREVIATIONS

MP (make picot): ch2, sl st in second ch from hook.

BORDER

Round 1: Work a second sc in last st of prev row (corner made), work 1sc in each row end down left-hand side, 2sc in corner st, work 1sc in each st along bottom edge, 2sc in corner st, work 1sc in each row end up right-hand side, 2sc in corner st, sl st in first st of last row of pillow to join.
Fasten off.

Pillow cover lower back

(make 1)
Using US size H/8 (5mm) hook and A, ch71.
Row 1: 1sc in second ch from hook, 1 sc in each ch to end, turn. *(70 sts)*
Row 2: Ch1 (does not count as st), 1sc in each st to end, turn.
Rep Row 2 until work measures 9¼in (23.5cm).

BORDER

Round 1: Work a second sc in last st of prev row (corner made), work 1sc in each row end down left-hand side, 2sc in corner st, work 1sc in each st along bottom edge, 2sc in corner st, work 1sc in each row end up right-hand side, 2sc in corner st, sl st in first st of last row of pillow to join.
Fasten off.

Mistletoe sprigs

(make 10)
Using US size E/4 (3.5mm) hook and B, ch11.
Leaf 1: Sl st in second ch from hook, sl st in each of next 3 ch, 1sc in each of next 4 ch, 1hdc in next ch, 2hdc in last ch, working down opposite side of ch, 1hdc in each of next 4 ch, 1sc in each of next 3 ch, sl st in each of last 2 ch.
Stalk: Ch8, sl st in second ch from hook, sl st back to base of Leaf 1.
Leaf 2: Ch9, 1hdc in second ch from hook, 1hdc in each of next 2 ch, 1sc in each of next 3 ch, sl st in each of last 2 ch, working down opposite side of ch, sl st in each of next 3 ch, 1sc in each of next 3 ch, sl st in next ch, sl st in top of first st to join.
Fasten off.

Holly leaves

(make 10)
Using US size E/4 (3.5mm) hook and C, ch12.
Round 1: 1sc in second ch from hook, 1sc in next ch, 1hdc in each of next 2 ch, 1dc in each of next 2 ch, 1hdc in each of next 3 ch, 1sc in each of last 2 ch, working down opposite side of ch, 1sc in each of next 3 ch, 1hdc in next 2 ch, 1dc in each of next 2 ch, 1hdc in each of next 2 ch, 1sc in last ch. 21 sts.
Stalk: Ch6, sl st in second ch from hook, sl st in each ch back to base of leaf.
Round 2: Sl st in first st, MP, sl st in next st, [1sc in next st, MP, sl st in next st] 4 times, (1sc, ch3, sl st in third ch from hook, sl st) in next st, working down opposite side of leaf, sl st in next st, [MP, sl st in next st, 1sc in next st] 4 times, sl st in next st, sl st in base of leaf to join.
Fasten off.

Holly berries

(make 14)
Using US size B/1-C/2 (2.5mm) hook and D, make a magic ring.
Round 1: 4sc in ring. *(4 sts)*
Round 2: [1sc in next st, 2sc in next st] twice, sl st in first sc to join. *(6 sts)*
Fasten off leaving a long yarn tail.
Use the yarn tail to close each holly berry at the back by running a gathering thread around the base and pulling it up tightly.

Making up and finishing

Sew in ends on the pillow cover. Lay the pillow cover front on a flat surface, RS down. Place the pillow cover upper back and lower back on top of the front piece so that the two back edges overlap, with RS up. Pin across the join at the back of the pillow where the opening will be. Pin the pompom edging all the way around the pillow edges, making sure that the front and back pieces are all joined. Using a sewing needle and thread, stitch the sides together all the way around the pillow.
Turn the pillow over so that the RS is facing you and place the pillow pad inside the cover. Position the leaves where you want them to be for the wreath and hold in place with safety pins. Slide the pillow pad out. Slide a piece of cardboard inside to

avoid the front and back of the pillow getting stitched together. Using a sewing needle and thread, stitch the leaves securely in place. Stitch the holly berries in place. Stitch the red velvet bow in place at the top of the wreath. Using a yarn needle threaded with E, work two or three French knots for mistletoe berries where the two leaves of each mistletoe sprig join.

Remove the cardboard and insert the pillow pad.

Stitch the three snap fasteners into place so that the opening of the pillow is closed, and the fasteners are hidden underneath the overlapping flap. Using a sewing needle and thread, sew the three buttons onto the back of the pillow, directly above where the fasteners are.

Mistletoe Pillow

The bright red and green on this pillow instantly create such a classic festive feel, and who can resist a bunch of mistletoe? The cover is worked as one piece and has a simple overlap opening at the back.

SKILL LEVEL ●●

YARN AND MATERIALS

King Cole Fashion (70% acrylic, 30% wool) worsted (Aran) weight yarn, 219yd (200m) per 3½oz (100g) ball
3 balls in Granary 089 (A)

Cascade Yarns 220 Superwash (100% merino wool) light worsted (DK) weight yarn, 219yd (200m) per 3½oz (100g) ball
1 ball in Peridot 286 (B)

Cascade Yarns Heritage (75% merino wool, 25% nylon) sport (4-ply) weight yarn, 437yd (400m) per 3½oz (100g) ball
1 ball in Snow 5618 (C)

Lion Brand Heartland (100% acrylic) worsted (Aran) weight yarn, 252yd (230m) per 5oz (140g) ball
1 ball in Redwood 113 (D)

Sewing thread

12 x 12in (30 x 30cm) pillow pad

20in (50cm) of ⅜in (10mm) wide ribbon in co-ordinating color

HOOKS AND EQUIPMENT

US size 7 (4.5mm), US size E/4 (3.5mm), and US size C/2-D/3 (3mm) crochet hooks

Yarn needle

Stitch marker

12 x 12in (30 x 30cm) piece of cardboard

Safety pins

Sewing needle

FINISHED MEASUREMENTS

Approx. 14¾ x 14¾in (35.5 x 35.5cm)

GAUGE (TENSION)

16 sts x 15 rows = 4 x 4in (10 x 10cm) working half double crochet between stitches, using a US size 7 (4.5mm) hook and King Cole Fashion.

ABBREVIATIONS

See page 127.

For the pillow cover

(make 1)

Using a US size 7 (4.5mm) hook and A, ch126.

Row 1 (RS): 1hdc in second ch from hook, 1hdc in each ch to end, turn. *(125 sts)*

Row 2: Ch2 (counts as first hdc), *1hdc in space between next 2 hdc, rep from * to end, turn. *(125 sts)*

Rep Row 2 until work measures 12½in (32cm).

Fasten off and sew in ends.

For the mistletoe

(make 2 of each branchlet)

FIRST BRANCHLET (LEAVES 1 TO 4)

Using a US size E/4 (3.5mm) hook and B, ch9.

Leaf 1: Starting in second ch from hook, work 4dc, 2hdc, 1sc, sl st.

Leaf 2: Ch10, starting in second ch from hook, work 4dc, 4hdc, sl st.

Stalk 1: Ch10, PM in last ch, ch12 (for stalk 2), ch12 (for Leaf 3).

Leaf 3: Starting in third ch from hook, work, 2tr, 3dc, 3hdc, 2sc, sl st.

Leaf 4: Ch12, starting in third ch from hook, work 2tr, 3dc, 2hdc, 2sc, sl st, sl st back in base of Leaf 3.

Fasten off.

Stalk 3: Join in yarn at marker, ch14.

Fasten off.

SECOND BRANCHLET (LEAVES 5 TO 9)

Using a US size E/4 (3.5mm) hook and B, ch8.

Leaf 5: Starting in second ch from hook, work, 3dc, 3hdc, 1sc.

Leaf 6: Ch9, starting in second ch from hook, work 2dc, 2hdc, 2sc, sl st, sl st back in top of Leaf 5.

Stalk 4: Ch6, PM in last ch.

Stalk 5: Ch12, ch10 (for Leaf 7).

Leaf 7: Starting in third ch from hook, work 3tr, 3dc, 1hdc, sl st.

Leaf 8: Ch12, starting in third ch from hook, work 4tr, 3dc, 1hdc, 1sc, sl st back in base of Leaf 7. Fasten off B.

Leaf 9: Join in B at marker, leave marker in place, ch9, starting in second ch from hook, work 3dc, 2hdc, 3sc, sl st.

Stalk 6: Ch12, join in first branchlet, ch16 for main stalk that connects branchlets, starting in second ch from hook, work 1hdc, 14sc.

NOTE

To give a denser fabric, the blanket is worked in half double crochet but with each stitch being worked into the space between the stitches from the row below, rather than into the loops of the stitch itself. Take care to insert the hook into the correct place as indicated by pattern and to maintain the correct stitch count throughout.

Fasten off B.
Join in B at start of first branchlet and work sl st in each st of stalk, then sl st around Leaves 1 and 2, finishing off at top of Leaf 2.
Join in B at fork in branch above Leaves 1 and 2, sl st down stalk and around Leaves 3 and 4, increasing around leaf tips as described in Tip.
Fasten off B at top of Leaf 4.
Sew in all ends on Branchlet 1.
Join in B at start of Branchlet 2, sl st down stalk and around Leaves 5 and 6, increasing as described in Tip. Sl st back up stalk, down second stalk of Branchlet 2, and around Leaves 7 and 8.
Fasten off B.
Join in B at Leaf 9 and sl st around.
Fasten off B and sew in all ends.

For the berries

(make 10)
Using a US size C/2-D/3 (3mm) hook and C, make a magic ring.
Round 1: 4sc into ring.
Round 2: [1sc, 2sc in next st] twice. *(6 sts)*
Round 3: [2sc, 2sc in next st] twice. *(8 sts)*
Fasten off.
Stuff berry with starting yarn tail and sew up opening, leaving a yarn tail.

Making up and finishing

Lay the front pillow panel, with the longest length on the vertical, on a flat surface, RS down. Place the pillow pad in the middle and fold the bottom of the cover up and the top of the cover down, to make an overlapping opening. Pin the side edges together. With the front of the pillow facing, join in A and work a single crochet seam down each side of the pillow to join the all the edges together.
Fasten off A.

FOR THE SIDE EDGING

With RS facing and using a US size E/4 (3.5mm) hook, join in D at the start of one edge.
Row 1: Ch1, 1sc in each row end to end, turn.
Row 2: Ch1, 3sc in each st to end.
Fasten off and sew in ends.
Rep edging on other side of pillow.
Take the pad out of the pillow and slide the cardboard in so that, when sewing on the mistletoe, the front and back do not get sewn together. With the RS of the pillow facing, position the Mistletoe where you want it and pin in place with safety pins. Use a needle and thread to stitch it securely in place. Using the yarn tail left on each berry, attach the berries. Remove the cardboard and insert the pillow pad. Thread a strip of the ribbon above the stalks to create a "hanging" ribbon. Make a bow and sew securely to the front of the bunch.

TIP
As you are working the slip stitch around each leaf tip, work 2 slip stitches into the stitches around the curves so that the leaves do not lose their shape. When working 2 slip stitches into the same stitch, work the first slip stitch into both loops and the second slip stitch into the back loop only.

Holly Blanket

Sometimes, less is more, and this Christmas blanket is wonderfully, but quietly, festive. With a single crochet background worked in worsted (Aran) weight yarn, the blanket is quick to make, and the holly leaves and berries, which have the tiniest of sparkles, are combined with a simple red ruffle edging to add the smallest of finishing touches.

SKILL LEVEL ●

YARN AND MATERIALS

King Cole Fashion (70% acrylic, 30% wool) worsted (Aran) weight yarn, 219yd (200m) per 3½oz (100g) ball
 9 balls in Granary 089 (A)

Lion Brand Heartland (100% acrylic) worsted (Aran) weight yarn, 252yd (230m) per 5oz (140g) ball
 2 balls in Redwood 113 (B)

Cascade Yarns 220 Superwash (100% merino wool) light worsted (DK) weight yarn, 219yd (200m) per 3½oz (100g) ball
 1 ball in Hunter Green 1950 (C)

Anchor Artiste Metallic (80% viscose, 20% polyester) thread, 109yd (100m) per ⅞oz (25g) ball
 1 ball in each of:
 Green 322 (D)
 Red 318 (E)

Sewing thread

HOOKS AND EQUIPMENT

US size H/8 (5mm) and US size E/4 (3.5mm) crochet hooks

Yarn needle

Sewing needle

Safety pins

Blocking pins

FINISHED MEASUREMENTS

Blanket: 44 x 43¾in (112 x 111cm)

Leaves: 4in (10cm)

GAUGE (TENSION)

16 sts x 20 rows = 4 x 4in (10 x 10cm) working single crochet, using a US size H/8 (5mm) hook and King Cole Fashion.

ABBREVIATIONS

See page 127.

For the blanket

Using a US size H/8 (5mm) hook and A, ch175.

Row 1 (RS): 1sc in second ch from hook, 1sc in each ch to end, turn. *(174 sts)*

Row 2: Ch1 (does not count as a st throughout), 174sc, turn.

Rep Row 2 until work measures 42½in (108cm), ending with a RS row.

FOR THE BORDER

Round 1: Ch1, [1sc in each row end to corner, 3sc in corner, 1sc in each st to corner, 3sc in corner] twice, sl st in beg st to join.

Fasten off A and sew in ends.

Round 2: Join B, ch1, 3sc in each st all around blanket, sl st in beg st to join.

Round 3: Ch1, 2sc in each st all around the blanket, sl st in beg st to join.

Fasten off and sew in ends.

For the holly leaves

(make 18 in C and D, 1 strand of each held together)

Using a US size E/4 (3.5mm) hook and 1 strand each of C and D, ch14.

Round 1: 1sc in second ch from hook, 1sc in next ch, 3hdc, 4dc, 3hdc, 3sc in last ch, working down opposite side of ch, 3hdc, 4dc, 3hdc, 2sc, ch5 for stalk, 1sc in second ch from hook, 3sl st.

Round 2: Sl st back into first st at start of Round 1, 1sc in same st.

Point 1: 1hdc in next st, ch3, 1sc in second ch from hook, 1hdc in next ch, skip 1 st from Round 1, sl st in next st.

Point 2: 1hdc in next st, ch4, sl st in second ch from hook, 1sc, 1hdc in next ch, skip 1 st from Round 1, sl st in next st.

Point 3: 1hdc in next st, ch4, sl st in second ch from hook, 1sc, 1hdc in next ch, skip 1 st from Round 1, sl st in next st.

Point 4: 1sc in next st, ch3, 1sc in second ch from hook, 1hdc in next ch, skip 1 st from Round 1, [sl st in next st] twice.

Point 5: Sl st in next st, ch3, sl st in second ch from hook, 1sc in next ch, sl st in next st from Round 1.

Working down opposite side of leaf:

Point 6: Sl st in next st, ch2, 1sc in second ch from hook, skip 1 st from Round 1, sl st in next st.

Point 7: 1sc in next st, ch3, sl st in second ch from hook, 1sc in next ch, skip 1 st from Round 1, sl st in next st.

Point 8: 1sc in next st, ch3, sl st in second ch from hook, 1sc in next ch, skip 1 st from Round 1, sl st in next st.

Point 9: 1sc in next st, ch3, sl st in second ch from hook, 1sc in next ch, skip 1 st from Round 1, sl st in next st.

Fasten off and sew in ends.

For the berries

(make 18 in B and E, 1 strand of each held together)

Using a US size E/4 (3.5mm) hook and 1 strand each of B and E, make a magic ring.

Round 1: 4sc into ring, do not join, cont working in a spiral. *(4 sts)*

Round 2: [2sc in next st, 1sc] twice. *(6 sts)*

Round 3: 5sl st.

Fasten off.

Stuff berry with yarn ends and sew up remaining opening.

Making up and finishing

Stitch one holly berry to each holly leaf.

Lay the blanket on a flat surface, RS up. Position the leaves where you want them and hold in place with safety pins.

Using a sewing needle and thread, stitch the pieces securely into place.

Block the blanket by pinning it onto foam matting or a towel with blocking pins. Spray lightly with water and allow to air dry.

Square Storage Basket

This fun storage solution is made from recycled T-shirt yarn. Working with two strands of the yarn and an 8mm crochet hook, you can make it in no time at all and it is perfect for storing Christmas presents, ready for the big day.

SKILL LEVEL ●

YARN AND MATERIALS

Paintbox Yarns Recycled T-Shirt (90% cotton, 10% synthetic) super bulky (super chunky) weight yarn, 120yd (110m) per 28¼oz (800g) ball

3 balls of Off White shade 003 (A)

Hobbii Ribbon (100% cotton) super bulky (super chunky) weight yarn, approx. 136yd (125m) per 8¾oz (250g) ball

1 cone of Egg Yolk shade 36 (B)

HOOKS AND EQUIPMENT

US size L/11 (8mm) crochet hook

US size J/10 (6mm) crochet hook

Large pins/safety pins

Large yarn needle

Locking stitch marker

Sewing needle and thread

FINISHED MEASUREMENTS

Width 13¾in (35cm), length 13¾in (35cm), depth 10¼in (26cm)

GAUGE (TENSION)

5 sts x 5 rows = 3¾ x 3¾in (9.5 x 9.5cm) working single crochet, using a US size L/11 (8mm) crochet hook and 2 strands of Paintbox Yarns Recycled T-Shirt held together.

ABBREVIATIONS

See page 127.

Basket

BASE

Using US size L/11 (8mm) hook and 2 strands of A held tog, ch17.

Row 1: 1sc in second ch from hook, 1sc in each ch to end, turn. *(16 sts)*

Row 2: Ch1 (does not count as st throughout), 1sc in each st to end, turn.

Rows 3–15: Rep Row 2.

Row 16: Ch1, 1sc in each st to last st, (1sc, 1ch, 1sc) in last st, cont down left-hand side 15sc evenly to corner, (1sc, 1ch, 1sc) in corner, 1sc in each st along bottom edge to last st, (1sc, 1ch, 1sc) in last st, work 15sc evenly up right-hand side to corner, (1sc, 1ch, 1sc) in corner, sl st in top of ch-1 to join. *(68 sts)*

Fasten off.

SIDES

With RS facing, using US size L/11 (8mm) hook and 2 strands of A held tog, join yarn in any sc immediately to the left of a ch-1 sp.

Row 1: Ch1, 1sc BLO in each of next 17 sts, turn. *(17 sts)*

Row 2: Ch1, working in both loops, 1sc in each of 17 sts, turn.

Rows 3–15: Rep Row 2.

Fasten off.

Rep on other sides of base to work other 3 sides.

HANDLES

(make 2)

Using US size L/11 (8mm) hook and 2 strands of A held tog, ch36.

Row 1: 1sc in second ch from hook, 1sc in each ch to end. *(35 sts)*

Fasten off.

Star

(make 4)

Using US size J/10 (6mm) hook and B, make a magic ring.

Round 1: 5sc in ring. *(5 sts)*

Work in a continuous spiral. PM in last st and move up as each round is finished.

Round 2: 2sc in each st to end. *(10 sts)*

Round 3: [1sc in next st, 2sc in next st] 5 times. *(15 sts)*

Round 4: [1sc in each of next 2 sts, 2sc in next st] 5 times. *(20 sts)*

Round 5: *Ch6, sl st in second ch from hook, 1sc in next ch, 1hdc in next ch, 1dc in next ch, 1tr in next ch, miss 3 sts on central circle, sl st in next st; rep from * 4 times to make 5 points in total, sl st in base of first point to join.

Fasten off.

Making up and finishing

With the RS of the base facing down, fold the four sides of the basket up and pin together with large pins or safety pins. Work a sc seam down each of the four corners.

Fasten off.
Thread the handle ends through from the outside to the inside of the basket, approximately one row down and six stitches apart, on opposite sides of the basket. Tie a large knot at each end to hold the handle in place.
Using a sewing needle and thread, stitch one star onto the center of each side.
Using US size J/10 (6mm) hook and B, work 2sc in each st around the top edge.
Fasten off. Sew in any ends.

TIP

As the main yarn is quite bulky, when finishing off your ends, you may find it easier to use a small crochet hook to pull all the ends to the inside of the basket and tie them off. Loose ends can then be woven underneath the inside stitches with a crochet hook.

Christmas Wreath Place Settings

For something a little different, why not make all of your Christmas dinner guests a mini festive wreath? They are very quick to complete and can be personalized with individual name tags.

SKILL LEVEL •

YARN AND MATERIALS

For eight mini wreaths:

DMC Natura XL (100% cotton) super bulky (super chunky) weight yarn, 82yd (75m) per 3½oz (100g) ball

1 ball of shade 72 (A)

Cascade Yarns Ultra Pima Fine (100% cotton) sport (5-ply) weight yarn, 137yd (125m) per 1¾oz (50g) ball

1 ball each of:

Emerald shade 3737 (B)

Paprika shade 3771 (C)

8 wooden rings, 2¾in (70mm) diameter

8 gold craft jingle bells, ⅞in (20mm) size

8 small cardboard name tags

Approx. 1yd (1m) of ⅜in (10mm) wide red gingham ribbon

HOOKS AND EQUIPMENT

US size J/10 (6mm) and US size 0 (2mm) crochet hooks

Yarn needle

Hot glue gun

FINISHED MEASUREMENTS

3¼in (8cm) diameter

GAUGE (TENSION)

5 sts x 5 rows = 1½ x 2in (4 x 5cm) working single crochet, using a US size J/10 (6mm) crochet hook and DMC Natura XL.

15 sts x 15 rows = 2¼ x 2⅜in (5.5 x 6cm) working single crochet, using a US size 0 (2mm) crochet hook and Cascade Yarns Ultra Pima Fine.

ABBREVIATIONS

See page 127.

SPECIAL ABBREVIATIONS

MP (make picot): ch2, sl st in second ch from hook.

Wreath

(make 8)

Attach A to the wooden ring with a knot.

Using US size J/10 (6mm) hook, work sc all around the ring, sl st in top of first sc to join.

Fasten off, leaving a long yarn tail.

Holly leaf

(make 16)

Using US size 0 (2mm) hook and B, ch6.

Sl st in second ch from hook, [MP, sl st in next st] 3 times, sl st in next st, MP (tip made), working down opposite side of ch, sl st in next st, [MP, sl st in next st] twice, sl st in next st.

Fasten off.

Making up and finishing

Using a yarn needle threaded with C, work two or three French knots (see page 125) at the base of each leaf for the berries. Thread a bell onto the long yarn tail left at the end of the wreath, and then sew in the yarn tail to secure at the back of the wreath.

Fasten off.

Use a hot glue gun to stick two holly leaves at the base of each wreath. Make small bows in gingham ribbon and glue at the top of each wreath. Tie on a name tag.

Christmas Greenery Place Settings

With all the many colors around during the holidays, these green and white sprigs will add a little natural calm to your Christmas table. Tie a name tag to each one to make them beautifully personal.

SKILL LEVEL ●●

YARN AND MATERIALS

Cascade Yarns Heritage (75% merino wool, 25% nylon) sport (4-ply) weight yarn, 437yd (400m) per 3½oz (100g) ball
 1 ball in each of:
 Moss 5612 (A)
 Snow 5618 (C)

Cascade Yarns Ultra Pima (100% cotton) light worsted (DK) weight yarn, 219yd (200m) per 3½oz (100g) ball
 1 ball of Sage 3720 (B)

Packet of 14in (35.5cm) 26-gauge floral stem wire

Roll of florist's green stem tape

Short twig, approx. 5½in (14cm) long per sprig

Short length of ribbon per sprig

Sewing thread

HOOKS AND EQUIPMENT

US size E/4 (3.5mm) and US size B/1-C/2 (2.5mm) crochet hooks

Stitch marker

Yarn needle

Blocking pins

Spray starch

Sewing needle

Hot glue gun

FINISHED MEASUREMENTS

6in (15cm) long

GAUGE (TENSION)

Exact gauge (tension) is not essential on this project.

ABBREVIATIONS

See page 127.

For the large eucalyptus leaves

(make 3 per sprig)

Using a US size E/4 (3.5mm) hook and B, make a magic ring.

Round 1: 6sc into ring. *(6 sts)*

Pull up closing yarn tail to form a semi-circle, sl st into ring.

Round 2: (1sc, 1hdc) in first st, (1hdc, 1dc) in next st, (1dc, 1tr) in next st, (1tr, 1dc) in next st, (1dc, 1hdc) in next st, (1hdc, 1sc) in next st, sl st in beg sc to join.

Close ring, fasten off, and sew in ends.

For the medium eucalyptus leaves

(make 2 per sprig)

Using a US size E/4 (3.5mm) hook and B, make a magic ring.

Round 1: 5sc into ring. *(5 sts)*

Pull up closing yarn tail to form a semi-circle, sl st into ring.

Round 2: (Sl st, 1sc) in first st, (1sc, 1hdc) in next st, 2dc in next st, (1hdc, 1sc) in next st, (1sc, sl st) in the next st.

Close ring, fasten off, and sew in ends.

NOTE

Each place setting has a eucalyptus sprig made up of three large leaves, two medium leaves, and two small leaves, plus one sprig of fir and nine snowberries.

For the small eucalyptus leaves

(make 2 per sprig)

Using a US size E/4 (3.5mm) hook and B, make a magic ring.

Round 1: 4sc into ring. *(4 sts)*

Pull up closing yarn tail to form a semi-circle, sl st into ring.

Round 2: Sl st in first st, (1sc, 1hdc) in next st, (1hdc, 1sc) in next st, sl st in next st.

Close ring, fasten off, and sew in ends.

For the fir

(make 1 per sprig)

Using a US size E/4 (3.5mm) hook and A, ch35.

Round 1: Sl st in second ch from hook, sl st in each of next 19 ch.

FOR THE FRONDS

Frond 2: [Ch8, sl st in second ch from hook, 6sl st, sl st in next st on main ch] twice.

Frond 3: [Ch7, sl st in second ch from hook, 5sl st, sl st in next st on main ch] 3 times.

Frond 4: [Ch6, sl st in second ch from hook, 4sl st, sl st in next st on main ch] 4 times.

Frond 5: [Ch5, sl st in second ch from hook, 3sl st, sl st in next st on main ch] 5 times.

Ch5, sl st in second ch from hook, 3sl st, sl st in same starting st.

Work down opposite side of original ch as follows:

Rep Frond 5 five times.

Rep Frond 4 four times.

Rep Frond 3 three times.

Rep Frond 2 twice.

Fasten off and sew in ends.

For the snow berries

(make 9 per sprig)

Work in a continuous spiral, PM at end of each round and move up as each round is finished.

Using a US size B/1-C/2 (2.5mm) hook and C, make a magic ring.

Round 1: 5sc into ring. *(5 sts)*

Round 2: [2sc in next st] 5 times. *(10 sts)*

Round 3: 10sc.

Round 4: [Sc2tog] 5 times, stuff with yarn ends. *(5 sts)*

Close ring, fasten off, and sew in ends.

Making up and finishing

Block all the eucalyptus leaves and the fir and leave to air dry. Bend a stem wire in half. Thread a large leaf onto the wire, right up to the bend. Take two further large leaves and thread each one onto one of the two wire halves. Twist the two wires below the two leaves. Thread on the two medium leaves in the same way and twist the wire underneath them. Thread on the two small leaves in the same way. Twist the two wires together below the small leaves make one stem. Cover the wire stem with florist's tape.

Sew a piece of stem wire down the center back of the main spine of each piece of fir. Trim the wire to match the length of the stem.

Use the hot glue gun to stick the snowberries onto the twig. Arrange the three items into a sprig and hold in place with some stem wire.

Cover the wire binding with the ribbon and tie securely.

Hot Water Bottle Cover

Nothing quite beats snuggling up with a hot water bottle on a cold night—and when it's tucked inside this cozy cover, both you and the hot water bottle will stay toasty and warm for hours. Worked as a simple rectangle, the cover is a generous fit for all standard-sized hot water bottles.

SKILL LEVEL ●●●

YARN AND MATERIALS

Debbie Bliss Baby Cashmerino (55% wool, 33% acrylic, 12% cashmere) sport (5-ply) weight yarn, 137yd (125m) per 1¾oz (50g) ball

2 balls each of:
Flame shade 306 (A)
Mustard shade 316 (D)
1 ball each of:
Camel shade 102 (B)
White shade 100 (C)

19¾in (50cm) of ⅞in (22mm) wide coordinating ribbon

1 hot water bottle, standard size

HOOKS AND EQUIPMENT

US size E/4 (3.5mm) crochet hook

Yarn needle

FINISHED MEASUREMENTS

Width 8¼in (21cm), length 15in (38cm)

GAUGE (TENSION)

15 sts x 15 rows = 2½ x 23/8in (6.5 x 6cm) working single crochet, using a US size E/4 (3.5mm) crochet hook.

ABBREVIATIONS

See page 127.

SPECIAL ABBREVIATIONS

MB (make bobble): using yarn that is laid along top of row, [yarn over hook, insert hook in stitch, yarn over hook, pull yarn through work, yarn over hook, pull yarn through first 2 loops on hook] 4 times all in same stitch, using main color yarn over hook, pull through all loops on hook.

Cover

Using US size E/4 (3.5mm) hook and A, ch91.

Row 1: 1sc in second ch from hook, 1sc in each ch to end. *(90 sts)*

Turn at end of this row and every foll row. Do not fasten off a yarn until instructed to do so, instead carry it loosely up the side between rows. Unless otherwise indicated, the color used for the first ch1 of each row should be used for the remainder of the row; join new colors when necessary.

Rows 2–4: Ch1 (does not count as st throughout), 1sc in each st to end.

Rows 5 and 6: Ch1 in D, 1sc in each st to end.

Row 7: Ch1 in A, 1sc in each st to end, fasten off A.

Row 8: Ch1 in B, 1sc in each st to end.

Row 9: Ch1 in B, lay D along top of row, 1sc in B in each of next sts, MB in D, *1sc in B in each of next 8 sts, MB in D; rep from * to last 4 sts, 1sc in B in each of last 4 sts.

Row 10: Ch1 in B, 1sc in each st to end, fasten off B.

Row 11: Ch1 in A, 1sc in each st to end, fasten off A.

Rows 12 and 13: Ch1 in D, 1sc in each st to end.

Row 14: Ch1 in C, lay B along top of row, *1sc in C in each of next 2 sts working yoh of last st in B, 1sc in B in each of next 2 sts working yoh of last st in C; rep from * to last 2 sts, 1sc in C in each of last 2 sts working yoh of last st in B.

Row 15: Ch1 in B, lay C along top of row, *1sc in B in each of next 2 sts working yoh of last st in C, 1sc in C in each of next 2 sts working yoh of last st in B; rep from * to last 2 sts, 1sc in B in each of last 2 sts, fasten off B and C.

Rows 16–18: Ch1 in A, 1sc in each st to end.

Row 19: Ch1 in D, 1sc in each st to end, fasten off D.

Row 20: Ch1 in B, 1sc in each st to end.

Row 21: Ch1 in B, lay A along top of row, 1sc in B in each of next 4 sts, MB in A, *1sc in B in each of next 8 sts, MB in A; rep from * to last 4 sts, 1sc in B in each of last 4 sts.

Row 22: Ch1 in B, 1sc in each st to end, fasten off B.

Row 23: Ch1 in D, 1sc in each st to end, fasten off D.

Rows 24 and 25: Ch1 in A, 1sc in each st to end, fasten off A.

Rows 26 and 27: Rep Rows 14 and 15.

Rows 28–30: Ch1 in D, 1sc in each st to end.

Row 31: Ch1 in A, 1sc in each st to end, fasten off A.

Row 32: Ch1 in B, 1sc in each st to end.

Row 33: Ch1 in B, lay D along top of row, 1sc in B in each of next 4 sts, MB in D, *1sc in B in each of next 8 sts, MB in D; rep from * to last 4 sts, 1sc in B in each of last 4 sts.

Row 34: Ch1 in B, 1sc in each st to end, fasten off B.

Row 35: Ch1 in A, 1sc in each st to end, fasten off A.

Rows 36 and 37: Ch1 in D, 1sc in each st to end, fasten off D.

Rows 38–61: Rep Rows 14–37.

Rows 62–83: Rep Rows 14–35.

Rows 84 and 85: Ch1 in D, 1sc in each st to end.

Row 86 (eyelet row): Ch1 in D, 1sc in each of next 5 sts, *ch3, miss next 3 sts, 1sc in each of next 4 sts; rep from * to last 8 sts, ch3, miss next 3 sts, 1sc in each of last 5 sts.

Rows 87–88: Ch1 in D, 1sc in each st to end.

Row 89: Join in C, ch1, lay B along top of row, *1sc in C in each of next 2 sts working yoh of last st in B, 1sc in B in each of next 2 sts working yoh of last st in C; rep from * to last 2 sts, 1sc in C in each of last 2 sts working yoh of last st in B.

Row 90: Ch1 in B, lay C along top of row, *1sc in B in each of next 2 sts working yoh of last st in C, 1sc in C in each of next 2 sts working yoh of last st in B; rep from * to last 2 sts, 1sc in B in each of last 2 sts, fasten off B and C.

Rows 91–94: Ch1 in A, 1sc in each st to end.

Row 95: Ch1 in D, 1sc in each st to end, fasten off D.

Row 96: Ch1 in B, 1sc in each st to end.

Row 97: Ch1 in B, lay A along top of row, 1sc in B in each of next 4 sts, MB in A, *1sc in B in each of next 8 sts, MB in A; rep from * to last 4 sts, 1sc in B in each of last 4 sts.

Row 98: Ch1 in B, 1sc in each st to end.

Row 99: Ch1 in D, 1sc in each st to end.

Rows 100 and 101: Ch1 in A, 1sc in each st to end, fasten off A.

Rows 102 and 103: Rep Rows 14 and 15.

Row 104: Ch1 in D, 1sc in each st to end.

Fasten off.

Making up and finishing

EDGING

With the RS of the work facing, using a US size E/4 (3.5mm) hook, join D in the top left-hand corner of the cover.

Row 1 (RS): Work 1sc in each row end down left-hand edge, turn.

Row 1 (WS): Ch1, 1sc in each st to end.

Fasten off.

Rep for the right-hand edge of the cover.

Sew in or knot together all ends on the inside of the cover.

With WS together and using D, join the two side edges together with a sc seam—this seam will be a feature on the center back of the cover. Center the sc seam on one side, turn the cover WS out, and sew the bottom edge closed. Turn RS out again.

Place the hot water bottle inside. Thread coordinating ribbon through the eyelets (Row 86), with the two ends meeting center front, and tie the ends in a bow.

Hellebore Candle Ring

When the rest of the garden is all very wintery and bare, the sight of hellebores poking out their heads ready for spring is such a lift to the spirits—and with this candle wreath, that pleasure can be brought indoors.

SKILL LEVEL ••

YARN AND MATERIALS

Cascade Yarns Heritage (75% merino wool, 25% nylon) sport (4-ply) weight yarn, 437yd (400m) per 3½oz (100g) ball

1 ball in each of:
- Snow 5618 (A)
- Wine 5663 (B)
- Herb 5658 (C)
- Primavera 5659 (D)

Packet of flower stamens (double-ended), 2⅜in (6cm) long

Sewing thread

Spray starch

8in (20cm) diameter wreath base

3 LED tealights/small candles

HOOKS AND EQUIPMENT

US size C/2-D/3 (3mm) and US size B/1-C/2 (2.5mm) crochet hooks

Yarn needle

Sewing needle

Blocking pins

Hot glue gun

FINISHED MEASUREMENTS

Diameter: 8in (20cm)

Hellebores: 2¾in (7cm)

GAUGE (TENSION)

32 sts x 38 rows = 4 x 4in (10 x 10cm) working single crochet, using a US size C/2-D/3 (3mm) hook and Cascade Yarns Heritage Superwash.

34 sts x 42 rows = 4 x 4in (10 x 10cm) working single crochet, using a US size B/1-C/2 (2.5mm) hook and Cascade Yarns Heritage Superwash.

Exact gauge (tension) is not essential on this project.

ABBREVIATIONS

See page 127.

For the flowers

(make 6 in A, 5 in B)

Using a US size C/2-D/3 (3mm) hook and either A or B, make a magic ring.

Round 1: 5sc into ring, sl st in beg st to join but do not completely close hole in center of ring.

Round 2: Ch1, [2sc in next st] 5 times. *(10 sts)*

Round 3: Ch1, [1sc, 2sc in next st] 5 times, sl st in beg st to join. *(15 sts)*

FOR THE PETALS

Change to a US size B/1-C/2 (2.5mm) hook.

Row 1: Ch1, 1scBLO in same st as ch1, 1scBLO in each of next 2 sts, ch1, turn. *(3 sts)*

Row 2: Ch1, [2sc in next st] 3 times, turn. *(6 sts)*

Row 3: Ch1, 2sc in first, 4sc, 2sc in last st, turn. *(8 sts)*

Rows 4 and 5: Ch1, 8sc, turn.

Row 6: Ch1, sc2tog, 4 sc, sc2tog, turn. *(6 sts)*
Row 7: Ch1, 6sc, turn.
Row 8: Ch1, [sc2tog] 3 times, turn. *(3 sts)*
Row 9: Ch1, sc3tog.
Fasten off.
Rejoin yarn with a sl stBLO to next st in Round 3.
Using a US size B/1–C/2 (2.5mm) hook, work 4 more petals as above.
Fasten off and sew in ends.

FOR THE EDGING

Using a US size C/2–D/3 (3mm) hook and A or C, join in with a sl st at any point of a petal.
Round 1: Work sc in row ends around edge of each petal, working 2sc if needed in curves to keep petal shape, work (1sc, 1ch, 1sc) all in same st at petal tips, at end of round sl st in beg st to join.
Fasten off and sew in ends.

For the leaf

(make 5 in C, 6 in D)
Each leaf is made up of three small leaves, all on one stalk.
Using a US size C/2–D/3 (3mm) hook and C or D, ch14.
Leaf 1: Starting in third ch from hook, 4dc, 4hdc, 3sc, sl st, 1ch, working down opposite side of ch, sl st, 3sc, 4hdc, 4dc, 2ch, sl st back in base of leaf.
Stalk: Ch6, 1sc in second ch from hook, 4sc back to leaf base, sl st back to base of leaf.
Leaf 2: Ch10, sl st in second ch from hook, 2sc, 4hdc, 5dc, 2tr, 1hdc, 1sc, ch2 across bottom, working down opposite side of ch, 1sc, 1hdc, 2tr, 5dc, 4hdc, 1sc, 2sl st.
Fasten off.
Leaf 3: Join in either C or D at center of stalk, ch14, sl st in second ch from hook, 3sc, 4hdc, 4dc, 1hdc, 1ch across bottom, working down opposite side of ch, 1hdc, 4dc, 4hdc, 1sc, 2sl st.
Fasten off and sew in ends.

FOR THE EDGING

Using a US size C/2–D/3 (3mm) hook and A or C, join in with a sl st at any point of a leaf.
Round 1: 1sc in each st around edge of each leaf, working (1sc, 1ch, 1sc) all in same st at each leaf tip, at end of round sl st in beg st to join.
Fasten off and sew in ends.

Making up and finishing

To finish off each leaf sprig, sew a couple of holding stitches into the leaf base, at the tip of the stalk, as this will give a firmer leaf.
For each flower, using the yarn needle and both C and D, work a couple of circles of French knots around the opening left from the magic ring.
Fold a few of the flower stamens in half and push the folded part through a hole left from the magic ring, from the RS through to the WS. Pull up and close the remaining hole on the magic ring and use a needle and thread to stitch the stamen stems in place on the underside of the flower. Repeat on each flower.
Block each flower and leaf, spraying with starch to give them a firmer body.
Lay the wreath base on a flat surface and position the flowers and leaves where you want them. Hold in place by pushing a pin through from the top of the piece into the wreath base. Using the hot glue gun, stick each piece in place securely.
Once complete, position the three candles in the center of the wreath.

Frosted Ivy Leaf Coasters

Is there anything more magical than seeing everything outside covered in a sparkling early morning frost? For me, these ivy leaf coasters create exactly that ethereal feeling, and what could be better than to use them for a glass of sparkling bubbly! The yarn amounts given are enough for four coasters.

For each coaster

Work in a continuous spiral.

Using a US size K/10½ (6.5mm) hook and A, make a magic ring.

Round 1: 5sc into ring.

Round 2: [2sc in next st] 5 times. *(10 sts)*

Round 3: [1 sc, 2sc in next st] 5 times. *(15 sts)*

Round 4:

Point 1: Ch3, 1sc in second ch from hook, 1hdc, skip 1 st from Round 3, sl st in next st.

Point 2: 1sc, ch4, 1 sc in second ch from hook, 1hdc, 1dc, skip 1 st from Round 3, sl st in next st.

Point 3: Ch7, 1sc in second ch from hook, 1hdc, 1dc, 1tr, 1ttr, skip 3 sts from Round 3, sl st in next st.

Point 4: Ch4, 1sc in second ch from hook, 1hdc, 1dc, skip 1 st from Round 3, 1sc in next st.

Point 5: Ch3, 1sc in second ch from hook, 1hdc, skip 1 st from Round 3, 1sc in next st.

Stalk: Ch6, 1hdc in third ch from hook, sl st in each ch back to leaf base.

Fasten off and sew in ends.

FOR THE EDGING

Using a US size G/6 (4mm) hook and B, join in yarn at any point of a leaf.

Round 1: 2sc in each st around edge of leaf, working (1sc, 1ch, 1sc) all in same st at leaf tips, at end of round sl st in beg st to join.

Fasten off and sew in ends.

Making up and finishing

Using a US size G/6 (4mm) hook and B, surface crochet the leaf veins out from the center to each leaf tip.

Block each coaster and leave to air dry.

SKILL LEVEL •

YARN AND MATERIALS

King Cole Big Value (100% acrylic) super bulky (super chunky) yarn, 89yd (81m) per 3½oz (100g) ball

1 ball in Glacier 1548 (A)

Rico Ricorumi Lamé (62% polyester, 38% nylon), 55yd (50m) per ⅜oz (10g) ball

1 ball in Silver 001 (B)

HOOKS AND EQUIPMENT

US size K/10½ (6.5mm) and US size G/6 (4mm) crochet hooks

Large yarn needle

Blocking pins

FINISHED MEASUREMENTS

5½in (14cm) long, 4¼in (11cm) wide

GAUGE (TENSION)

12 sts x 12 rows = 4 x 4in (10 x 10cm) working single crochet, using a US size K/10½ (6.5mm) hook and King Cole Big Value.

Exact gauge (tension) is not essential on this project.

ABBREVIATIONS

See page 127.

CHAPTER 3

Cards and GIFTS

Christmas Puddings and Snowballs

Make the gift of a simple wrapped chocolate into something special with these cute covers, designed as a snowball or as a Christmas pudding. They'd look great as decorations or favors on a festive table, too.

SKILL LEVEL ●●●

YARN AND MATERIALS

Rico Ricorumi Twinkly Twinkly (99% cotton) light worsted (DK) weight yarn, 1% polyester, approx. 62yd (57m) per ⅞oz (25g) ball
4 balls of Rainbow 002 (A)

Schachenmayr Catania (100% cotton) sport (5-ply) weight yarn, approx. 137yd (125m) per 1¾oz (50g) ball
1 ball each of shades:
Sun-Kissed 0437 (B)
Cinnamon 0383 (C)

Anchor Artiste Metallic (80% viscose, 20% polyester) thread, approx. 109yd (100m) per ⅞oz (25g) ball
1 ball each of shades:
Green 322 (D)
Red 318 (E)

HOOKS AND EQUIPMENT

US size B/1–C/2 (2.5mm) and US size B/1 (2mm) crochet hooks

Stitch marker

Yarn needle

FINISHED MEASUREMENTS

Each snowball/pudding: 5in (12.5cm) circumference

Each holly leaf: 1¼in (1.5cm) long

GAUGE (TENSION)

15 sts x 15 rows = 2¾ x 2⅜in (7 x 6cm) working single crochet, using a US size B/1–C/2 (2.5mm) crochet hook and Rico Ricorumi Twinkly Twinkly.

15 sts x 15 rows = 2⅜in (6cm) square working single crochet, using a US size B/1–C/2 (2.5mm) crochet hook and Schachenmayr Catania.

ABBREVIATIONS

See page 127.

For the covers

SNOWBALL BASE

Round 1: Using US size B/1–C/2 (2.5mm) hook and A, make a magic ring, 6sc into the ring.

Work in a continuous spiral. PM in last st and move up as each round is finished.

Round 2: 2sc in each st to end. *(12 sts)*

Round 3: *1sc, 2sc in next st; rep from * to end. *(18 sts)*

Round 4: *1sc in each of next 2 sts, 2sc in next st; rep from * to end. *(24 sts)*

Round 5: 1sc in each st to end.

Round 6: *1sc in each of next 3 sts, 2sc in next st; rep from * to end. *(30 sts)*

Rounds 7 and 8: 1sc in each st to end.

Join last round with a sl st in first st.

Fasten off.

SNOWBALL TOP

Round 1: Using US size B/1–C/2 (2.5mm) hook and A, make a magic ring, 6sc into the ring.

Work in a continuous spiral. PM in last st and move up as each round is finished.

Round 2: 2sc in each st to end. *(12 sts)*

Round 3: *1sc, 2sc in next st; rep from * to end. *(18 sts)*
Round 4: *1sc in each of next 2 sts, 2sc in next st; rep from * to end. *(24 sts)*
Round 5: 1sc in each st to end.
Round 6: *1sc in each of next 3 sts, 2sc in next st; rep from * to end. *(30 sts)*
Rounds 7 and 8: 1sc in each st to end.
Round 9: 1sc in each st to end, join with a sl st in first st.
Fasten off.

CHRISTMAS PUDDING BASE

Using US size B/1–C/2 (2.5mm) hook and B, work as for snowball base.

CHRISTMAS PUDDING TOP

Using US size B/1–C/2 (2.5mm) hook and A, work as for snowball top rounds 1 to 8.
Round 9: *(1hdc, 1dc) in next st, (1dc, 1hdc) in next st, sl st in each of next 2 sts; rep from * to end, ending final rep with (1dc, 1hdc, sl st) in last st, join with a sl st in first st.
Fasten off.

HOLLY LEAF

(make 2 per pudding/snowball)
Using US size B/1 (2mm) crochet hook and D, ch6.
Round 1: Sl st in 2nd ch from hook, [1hdc in next ch, sl st in next ch] twice, ch1 across bottom of leaf, do not turn, working back down other side of ch, sl st in each of next 2 ch, 1hdc in next ch, sl st in next ch, join with a sl st in first st.
Fasten off.

Making up and finishing

For each Christmas pudding/snowball, place a top and base around each chocolate. At the back of the cover, oversew a few stitches in yarn to create a hinge.
Sew two holly leaves to the top of each Christmas pudding/snowball. Using E, add French knots (see page 125) to create three holly berries between the leaves. Using C, add French knots to the base of each Christmas pudding.

Mistletoe Gift Bags

These little gift bags are perfect either for hanging on the Christmas tree or for marking everyone's places around the table. Each bag, worked in moss stitch in the round, has a simple drawstring ribbon around the top and is decorated with a sprig of mistletoe that hangs above a tiny red heart.

SKILL LEVEL ●●

YARN AND MATERIALS

Cascade Yarns Ultra Pima Fine (100% cotton) sport (4-ply) weight yarn, 137yd (125m) per 3½oz (100g) ball

1 ball in Silver 3801 (A)

Cascade Yarns Heritage (75% merino wool, 25% nylon) sport (4-ply) weight yarn, 437yd (400m) per 3½oz (100g) ball

1 ball in each of:
Christmas Red 5619 (B)
Herb 5658 (C)
Snow 5618 (D)

Sewing thread

16in (40cm) of ⅜in (10mm) wide ribbon per bag

HOOKS AND EQUIPMENT

US size E/4 (3.5mm), US size B/1–C/2 (2.5mm) and US size steel 4–B/1 (2mm) crochet hooks

Yarn needle

Safety pins

Sewing needle

FINISHED MEASUREMENTS

3 x 4¼in (7.5cm x 10.5cm)

GAUGE (TENSION)

27 sts x 28 rows = 4 x 4in (10 x 10cm) working single crochet cross st, using a US size E/4 (3.5mm) hook and Cascade Yarns Ultra Pima Fine.

ABBREVIATIONS

See page 127.

SPECIAL ABBREVIATIONS

sc cross st (single crochet cross stitch): insert hook in stitch, take yarn under hook, and pull yarn through st (2 loops on hook), yoh, and pull through both loops on hook.

For the bag

Using a US size E/4 (3.5mm) hook and A, ch40, sl st in beg ch to make a ring.

Round 1: Ch1 (does not count as a st throughout), sc cross st in same st as ch and in each ch to end, sl st in beg st to join. *(40 sts)*

Rounds 2 to 25: Rep Round 1.

Round 26: Ch1, [2sc cross st, ch2, skip 2 sts] all around, sl st in beg st to join.

Round 27: Ch1, [2sc cross st, 1sc in each of 2 ch from previous round] all around, sl st in beg st to join.

Round 28: Ch1, 40sc cross st, sl st in beg st to join.
Round 29: Ch2 (counts as hdc), 2hdc in st at base of ch2, 3hdc in each remaining st around, sl st in beg st to join. *(120 sts)*
Fasten off and sew in ends.

For the heart

(make 1 per bag)
Using a US size steel 4-B/1 (2mm) hook and B, ch14.
3sc in second ch from hook, 6sc, ch2, 1sc in same st as last sc, 5sc, 3sc in last st, working back down opposite side, 2sc in next ch, 3sc, miss 1 ch, sl st in next ch, miss 1 ch, 3sc, 2sc in next ch, sl st in beg st to join.
Fasten off and sew in ends.

For the mistletoe

(make 1 per bag)
Using a US size B/1-C/2 (2.5mm) hook and C, ch12.
Leaf 1: 1tr in third ch from hook, 1tr, 2dc, 2hdc, 4sc, ch11 for stem, 1sc in second ch from hook, 1sc in each ch back to base of Leaf 1.
Leaf 2: Ch12, 1tr in third ch from hook, 1tr, 2dc, 2hdc, 4sc, sl st in stalk to join.
Fasten off and sew in ends.

Making up and finishing

Bring the ends of the heart in slightly with RS facing to create a heart shape, and stitch a few stitches to pull the heart tips a little closer together.
Using a double strand of D and a yarn needle, work 3 French knots onto each leaf, just above the start of the stalk.
Turn the bag inside out and with the joining seam positioned down the center back, fold in half. Work a single crochet seam along the bottom edge to join together. Turn back RS out.
Place a small piece of cardboard inside the bag to avoid stitching the front and back together (optional). Position the heart and the mistletoe in place and pin with safety pins. Use a needle and thread to stitch the pieces in place.
Thread the ribbon through the holes around the top of the bag for the drawstring tie.

Bringing Home the Tree Card

There can be nothing more special than a handmade Christmas card. This crochet picture version can even be framed once received and brought out on subsequent years as a decoration. The background square is worked in simple single crochet stitch in a cotton light worsted (DK) weight yarn and then the car and tree are made separately and stitched on afterward. Again, only small quantities of yarn are needed, so this project is perfect for using up any leftover yarn that you may have to hand.

Background square

Using a US size D/3 (3mm) hook and A, ch24.

Row 1: Starting in second ch from hook, 1sc in back bump of each ch to end, turn. *(23 sts)*

Row 2: Ch1 (does not count as st), 1sc in each st to end, turn.

Rows 3–22: Rep Row 2.

Fasten off and sew in ends (see page 121).

Car body

Using a US size B/1–C/2 (2.5mm) hook and two strands of B held together, ch18.

Row 1: Starting in second ch from hook, 1sc in back bump of each ch to end, turn. *(17 sts)*

Row 2: Ch1 (does not count as st throughout), sc2tog, 1sc in each st to end, turn. *(16 sts)*

Row 3: Ch1, 1sc in each st to last 2 sts, sc2tog, turn. *(15 sts)*

Row 4: Ch1, 1sc in each st to last 2 sts, sc2tog, turn. *(14 sts)*

Row 5: Ch1, 1sc in each st to last 2 sts, sc2tog, turn. *(13 sts)*

Fasten off and sew in ends.

KEY POINTS

For a neat bottom edge to each square, see page 116 for details of working into the back bump of the starting chain.

As the crochet square is going to be behind the aperture in the card, there will be no need to work a finishing border.

I used two strands of fingering (4-ply) held together when making the car and the tree so one strand of light worsted (DK) weight would work equally as well. For the tree, I used strands of different color greens to add extra definition but one color would work equally well.

SKILL LEVEL ●●●

YARN AND MATERIALS

For the background square:

Cascade Yarns Ultra Pima (100% cotton) light worsted (DK) weight yarn, 220yd (200m) per 3½oz (100g) skein (hank)

1 skein of Gold 3747 (dark yellow) (A)

For the car and tree:

Cascade Yarns Heritage (75% merino wool, 25% nylon), fingering (4-ply) weight yarn, 437yd (400m) per 3½oz (100g) skein (hank)

Small amounts of:

Red shade 5607 (B)

White shade 5682 (C)

Charcoal shade 5631 (dark gray) (D)

Primavera shade 5659 (bright green) (E)

Cedar Green shade 5684 (dark green) (F)

Rico Ricorumi Lamé (62% polyester, 38% nylon) light worsted (DK) weight yarn, 54yd (50m) per ⅜oz (10g) ball

1 ball of Silver shade 001 (G)

4¾ x 4¾in (12 x 12cm) when folded tri-fold card blank, aperture size 3½ x 3½in (9 x 9cm)

Small twig for tree trunk

Silver glitter glue

Small piece of string or yarn

HOOKS AND EQUIPMENT

US size B/1-C/2 (2.5mm) crochet hook

US size C/2-D/3 (3mm) crochet hook

Stitch marker

Yarn needle

Sewing needle and thread

Hot glue gun

FINISHED MEASUREMENTS

Finished card: 4¾ x 4¾in (12 x 12cm)

Finished square approx. 3¾ x 3¾in (9.5 x 9.5cm)

GAUGE (TENSION)

25 sts x 28 rows = 4 x 4in (10 x 10cm) working single crochet using a US size D/3 (3mm) crochet hook and Cascade Yarns Ultra Pima.

ABBREVIATIONS

See page 127.

ROOF

With RS facing, count in 5 sts from top right-hand corner, join two strands of B held together in next st with a sl st, ch17. Starting in second ch from hook, 1sc in each ch back to original st on top edge, sew in ends where ch starts.
Making sure that roof piece is not twisted, sew other end to back edge of car.

EDGING

With RS facing and two strands of B held together, starting at bottom of roof at back of car, 1sc in each st and 2sc in any sts on a curve, all around car and over top of roof to beg of round, sl st in beg of round to join.
Fasten off and sew in ends.

WHEELS

Using a US size B/1–C/2 (2.5mm) hook and two strands of C held together, make a magic ring.
Round 1: 6sc into ring, sl st to join. *(6 sts)*
Fasten off C.
Round 2: Join two strands of D held together with a sl st and 2sc in same st, 2sc in each st around, sl st in beg of round to join. *(12 sts)*
Fasten off D and sew in ends.

Christmas tree

Worked in continuous rounds.
Using a US size B/1–C/2 (2.5mm) hook and one strand of E and one strand of F held together, make a magic ring.
Round 1: 4sc into ring.
Round 2: [1sc in next st, 2sc in next st] twice, PM for beg of round. *(6 sts)*
Round 3: [1sc in each of next 2 sts, 2sc in next st] twice. *(8 sts)*
Round 4: 1sc in each st.
Round 5: [1sc in each of next 3 sts, 2sc in next st] twice. *(10 sts)*
Round 6: 1sc in each st.
Round 7: [1sc in each of next 2 sts, 2sc in next st] 3 times, 1sc in last st. *(13 sts)*
Round 8: [1sc in each of next 3 sts, 2sc in next st] 3 times, 1sc in last st. *(16 sts)*
Round 9: [1sc in each of next 4 sts, 2sc in next st] 3 times, 1sc in last st. *(19 sts)*
Round 10: 1sc in each st.
Round 11: [1 sc in each of next 2 sts, 2sc in next st] 6 times, 1sc in last st. *(25 sts)*
Round 12: 1sc in each st.
Round 13: [1sc in each of next 5 sts, 2sc in next st] 4 times, 1sc in last st. *(29 sts)*
Fasten off and sew in ends.

Finishing

Place the background square inside the card mount. To allow room for the tree, place the car in position, very slightly over to the right rather than completely central, and sew in place with a sewing needle and thread. Using a length of B and a yarn needle, sew a couple of straight stitches (see page 125) from the underside of the roof down to the top edge of the car for the window divider. Stitch a square to indicate the car door. Using a length of D and a yarn needle, sew a couple of short straight stitches for the steering wheel and the exhaust, and work a French knot (see page 125) for a door handle. Sew the wheels in place with a sewing needle and thread.
Using G, work a few French knots onto the tree. Gently shape the tree so that the back is slightly pushed in toward the center to create a 3-D shape. Use a hot glue gun to stick the tree trunk inside the tree. Add a little glitter glue to the trunk.
Position the tree on top of the car and, using a yarn needle and either a piece of string or yarn, stitch around the tree to tie it to the roof of the car. Using a sewing needle and thread, sew the tree in place.
To finish, use C and a yarn needle to sew snow onto the square using French knots.
Add a few French knots in G among the snow and then a few along the ground underneath the car.
Finally, use a hot glue gun to stick the crochet square securely into the card mount.

Mistletoe Sprig Square

When the mistletoe comes out, the festive season has arrived! This little sprig has the tiniest of white bells for berries and is worked to create a 3-D effect so that the bunch stands out from the square. Each leaf and stem is worked individually, in the round, and then the stems are stitched together to finish.

SKILL LEVEL ●

YARN AND MATERIALS

For the background square:

Rowan Summerlite (100% cotton), fingering (4-ply) weight yarn, 191yd (175m) per 1¾oz (50g) ball

1 ball of Aqua shade 433 (turquoise) (A)

Cascade Yarns Ultra Pima (100% cotton) light worsted (DK) weight yarn, 220yd (200m) per 3½oz (100g) skein (hank)

Small amount of Lipstick Red shade 3755 (B)

For the mistletoe:

Rowan Summerlite (100% cotton), fingering (4-ply) weight yarn, 191yd (175m) per 1¾oz (50g) ball

Small amount of Mint shade 451 (light green)

4 small white craft bells

Small amount of red ribbon

Glitter glue (optional)

HOOKS AND EQUIPMENT

US size D/3 (3mm) crochet hook

US size B/1-C/2 (2.5mm) crochet hook

Yarn needle

Blocking pins and mat

Sewing needle and thread

FINISHED MEASUREMENTS

4 x 4in (10 x 10cm)

GAUGE (TENSION)

Exact gauge is not important for this project.

ABBREVIATIONS

See page 127.

Background square

Using a US size D/3 (3mm) hook and A, ch23.

Row 1: Starting in second ch from hook, 1sc in back bump of each ch to end, turn. *(22 sts)*

Row 2: Ch1 (does not count as st), 1sc in each st, turn.

Rows 3–22: Rep Row 2.

Fasten off.

EDGING

Round 1: Using a US size B/1-C/2 (2.5mm) hook and A, with RS facing join in yarn at center bottom of square with a sl st, 1sc in same st, *1sc in each st to corner, 3sc in corner st, 1sc in each row-end to next corner, 3sc in corner st; rep from * once more, 1sc in each st to beg of round, sl st to join.

Fasten off and sew in ends (see page 121).

Round 2: With RS facing, join B at center bottom with a sl stBLO, *sl stBLO in each of next 2 sts, ch3; rep from * to beg of round, sl st to join.

Fasten off and sew in ends.

Large mistletoe leaf

(make 3)

Using a US size B/1–C/2 (2.5mm) hook and Mint, make a magic ring.

Round 1: 4sc into ring. *(4 sts)*

Round 2: [1sc in next st, 2sc in next st] twice. *(6 sts)*

Round 3: 1sc in next st, 2sc in next st, 1 sc in each of next 3 sts, 2sc in next st. *(8 sts)*

Rounds 4–6: 1sc in each st.

Round 7: Sc2tog, 1sc in each of next 6 sts. *(7 sts)*

Round 8: Sc2tog, 1sc in each of next 5 sts. *(6 sts)*

Round 9: 1sc in each st.

Round 10: Sc2tog, 1sc in each of next 4 sts. *(5 sts)*

Round 11: 1sc in each st.

Round 12: [Sc2tog] twice, 1sc in next st, sl st to join. *(3 sts)*

Do not fasten off.

STEM

Row 1: Ch13, starting in second ch from hook, 1sc in each ch to end.

Fasten off.

Small mistletoe leaf

(make 3)

Using a US size B/1–C/2 (2.5mm) hook and Mint, make a magic ring.

Round 1: 4sc into ring. *(4 sts)*

Round 2: 2sc in next st, 1sc in each of next 3 sts. *(5 sts)*

Rounds 3–6: 1sc in each st.

Round 7: Sc2tog, 1sc in each of next 3 sts. *(4 sts)*

Round 8: [Sc2tog] twice. *(2 sts)*

Round 9: 1sc in each of next 2 sts, sl st to join.

Do not fasten off.

STEM

Row 1: Ch17, starting in second ch from hook, 1sc in each ch to end.

Fasten off.

Finishing

Block the square (see page 121).

Stitch the stems of one large and one small leaf together, with the curves of the leaves facing inward.

Position the three mistletoe sprigs on the square so that they make a bunch, with all the stems together/on top of each other.

Using a sewing needle and thread, stitch the one main stem to the square. If needed, stitch a couple of holding stitches at the base of the leaves to hold in position but keep the 3-D effect by not stitching all the way around.

Using a sewing needle and thread, sew the bells onto the mistletoe for berries.

Thread the ribbon into a yarn needle and thread each end from the back of the square to the front and then tie in a bow.

If needed, anchor the ends of the bow with a couple of holding stitches.

Paint some glitter glue onto the edges of the leaves to catch the light (optional).

Winter Penguin Square

Even penguins sometimes need to wrap up warm and this little one has his matching hat and scarf all ready for those snowy days. This square would be perfect for adding to some winter bunting or displayed in a box frame as a picture.

SKILL LEVEL ●●

YARN AND MATERIALS

For the background square:

Rowan Summerlite (100% cotton), fingering (4-ply) weight yarn, 191yd (175m) per 1¾oz (50g) ball

1 ball of Aqua shade 433 (turquoise) (A)

Cascade Yarns Ultra Pima (100% cotton) light worsted (DK) weight yarn, 220yd (200m) per 3½oz (100g) skein (hank)

Small amount of Lipstick Red shade 3755 (B)

For the penguin, hat, and scarf:

Cascade Yarns Heritage (75% merino wool, 25% nylon), fingering (4-ply) weight yarn, 437yd (400m) per 3½oz (100g) skein (hank)

Small amounts of:

Limestone shade 5681 (light gray)
Forged Iron shade 5736 (dark gray)
White shade 5682
Mustard shade 5652 (yellow)
Herb shade 5658 (green)
Red shade 5607

Pair of small back safety eyes

HOOKS AND EQUIPMENT

US size D/3 (3mm) crochet hook

US size B/1–C/2 (2.5mm) crochet hook

US steel size 4 (2mm) crochet hook

Yarn needle

Blocking pins and mat

Sewing needle and thread

FINISHED MEASUREMENTS

4 x 4in (10 x 10cm)

GAUGE (TENSION)

Exact gauge is not important for this project.

ABBREVIATIONS

See page 127.

Background square

Using a US size D/3 (3mm) hook and A, ch23.

Row 1: Starting in second ch from hook, 1sc in back bump of each ch to end, turn. *(22 sts)*

Row 2: Ch1 (does not count as st), 1sc in each st, turn.

Rows 3–22: Rep Row 2.

Fasten off.

EDGING

Round 1: Using a US size B/1–C/2 (2.5mm) hook and A, with RS facing join in yarn at center bottom of square with a sl st, 1sc in same st, *1sc in each st to corner, 3sc in corner st, 1sc in each row-end to next corner, 3sc in corner st; rep from * once more, 1sc in each st to beg of round, sl st to join.

Fasten off and sew in ends (see page 121).

Round 2: With RS facing, join B at center bottom with a sl st BLO, *sl stBLO in each of next 2 sts, ch3; rep from * to beg of round, sl st to join.

Fasten off and sew in ends.

Penguin body

Using a US size B/1–C/2 (2.5mm) hook and Limestone, make a magic ring.

Round 1: 6sc into ring. *(6 sts)*

Round 2: [2sc in next st] 6 times. *(12 sts)*

Round 3: [1sc in next st, 2sc in next st] 6 times. *(18 sts)*

Round 4: [1sc in each of next 2 sts, 2sc in next st] 6 times. *(24 sts)*

Round 5: [1sc in each of next 3 sts, 2sc in next st] 6 times. *(30 sts)*

Rounds 6–10: 1sc in each st.

Round 11: Sc2tog, 1sc in each of next 13 sts, sc2tog, 1sc in each of next 13 sts. *(28 sts)*

Round 12: Sc2tog, 1sc in each of next 12 sts, sc2tog, 1sc in each of next 12 sts. *(26 sts)*

Round 13: Sc2tog, 1sc in each of next 11 sts, sc2tog, 1sc in each of next 11 sts. *(24 sts)*

Round 14: 1sc in each st.

Fasten off Limestone, join in Forged Iron.

Rounds 15–17: 1sc in each st.

Round 18: Sc2tog, 1sc in each of next 10 sts, sc2tog, 1sc in each of next 10 sts. *(22 sts)*

Rounds 19–22: 1sc in each st.

Round 23: Sc2tog, 1sc in each of next 9 sts, sc2tog, 1sc in each of next 9 sts. *(20 sts)*

Round 24: [Sc2tog] 10 times. *(10 sts)*

Fasten off and sew up top.

Wings

(make 2)

Using a US size B/1–C/2 (2.5mm) hook and Forged Iron, make a magic ring.

Round 1: 4sc into ring. *(4 sts)*

Round 2: [1sc in next st, 2sc in next st] twice. *(6 sts)*

Rounds 3–9: 1sc in each st.

Fasten off.

Feet

(make 2)

Using a US size B/1–C/2 (2.5mm) hook and Forged Iron, ch5.

Round 1: Starting in second ch from hook, 1sc in each ch to last ch, 2sc in last ch, 1sc in each ch down opposite side of chain, 1sc in row-end. *(9 sts)*

Rounds 2 and 3: 1sc in each st.

At end of Round 3, sl st to join.

Fasten off.

Eyes

(make 1)

Using a US size B/1–C/2 (2.5mm) hook and White, ch10.

Row 1: Starting in second ch from hook, 1sc in each ch to end, turn. *(9 sts)*

Round 2: Ch1 (does not count as st), 1sc in next st, 1dc in next st, 1tr in next st, ch1, sl st in each of next 3 sts, ch1, 1tr in next st, 1dc in next st, 1sc in next st, do not turn, 1sc in each row-end down left-hand side, 1sc in each st along bottom edge, 1sc in each row-end up right-hand side, sl st to join.

Fasten off.

Beak

Using US steel size 4 (2mm) hook and Mustard, ch4.

Row 1: Starting in second ch from hook, 1sc in each ch to end, turn. *(3 sts)*

Row 2: Ch1 (does not count as st), sc2tog, 1sc in next st, turn. *(2 sts)*

Row 3: Sc2tog.

Fasten off.

Hat

Using a US size B/1–C/2 (2.5mm) hook and Herb, make a magic ring.

Round 1: 8sc into ring. *(8 sts)*

Round 2: Join in Red, leaving Herb at back, using Red [2sc in next st] 8 times. *(16 sts)*

Round 3: Bring up Herb, leaving Red at back, using Herb [1sc in next st, 2sc in next st] 8 times. *(24 sts)*

Round 4: Bring up Red, leaving Herb at back, using Red [1sc in each of next 2 sts, 2sc in next st] 8 times. *(32 sts)*

Round 5: Bring up Herb, leaving Red at back, using Herb 1sc in each st.

Fasten off Herb, cont in Red only.

Round 6: [1sc in each of next 14 sts, sc2tog] twice. *(30 sts)*

Rounds 7 and 8: 1sc in each st.

At end of Round 8, sl st to join.

Fasten off.

Scarf

Using a US size B/1–C/2 (2.5mm) hook and Red, ch46.

Row 1: Starting in second ch from hook, 1sc in each ch to end. *(45 sts)*

Fasten off.

Finishing

Block the square (see page 121).

Insert the two safety eyes into the center of each "eye arch" on the eyes piece. Sew the eyes piece onto the penguin.

Fold the beak triangle down the center from top edge to point to make a small beak shape. Use the yarn tails to secure.

Using a yarn needle and a doubled strand of Red work a large French knot (see page 125) at the top of the hat. To make the bobble bigger if required, oversew over the top of the French knot several times then fasten off.

Place the hat and scarf on the penguin and use a couple of stitches to secure.

Stitch the beak in to place just below and between the eyes.

Stitch the wings and feet onto the penguin using a sewing needle and thread.

Stitch the completed penguin onto the square.

Using White in a yarn needle, work French knots over the background and along the bottom of the square for snow.

Christmas Tree Square

This is a tree that is small enough to fit on anyone's mantelpiece and can be decorated as much or as little as you want. The glittery yarn used to create the boughs adds a festive twinkle, and with snow and glitter added around the base of the tree trunk, your Christmas scene is complete.

SKILL LEVEL ●●

YARN AND MATERIALS

For the background square:
Rowan Handknit Cotton (100% cotton) light worsted (DK) weight yarn, 92yd (85m) per 1¾oz (50g) ball
1 ball of Straw shade 381 (yellow) (A)
Small amount of Raspberry shade 356 (red) (B)

For the decoration:
Cascade Yarns Heritage (75% merino wool, 25% nylon), fingering (4-ply) weight yarn, 437yd (400m) per 3½oz (100g) skein (hank)
Small amounts of:
Sage shade 5635 (soft green) (C)
Herb shade 5658 (green) (D)
White shade 5682 (E)

Anchor Artiste Metallic (20% polyester, 80% viscose), fingering (4-ply) weight yarn, 109yd (100m) per ⅞oz (25g) ball
Small amount of Green shade 322 (F)

Small beads/stars/sequins

Short twig for trunk of tree

Glitter glue (optional)

HOOKS AND EQUIPMENT

US size E/4 (3.5mm) crochet hook

US size D/3 (3mm) crochet hook

US steel size 4 (2mm) crochet hook

Yarn needle

Blocking mat and pins

Hot glue gun

FINISHED MEASUREMENTS

3¾ x 3¾in (9.5 x 9.5cm)

GAUGE (TENSION)

Exact gauge is not important for this project.

ABBREVIATIONS

See page 127.

Background square

Using a US size E/4 (3.5mm) hook and A, ch17.

Row 1: Starting in second ch from hook, 1sc in back bump of each ch to end, turn. *(16 sts)*

Row 2: Ch1 (does not count as st), 1sc in each st, turn.

Rows 3–18: Rep Row 2.

Fasten off.

EDGING

Round 1: Using a US size D/3 (3mm) hook and A, with RS facing join in yarn at center bottom of square with a sl st, 1sc in same st, *1sc in each st to corner, 3sc in corner st, 1sc in each row-end to next corner, 3sc in corner st; rep from * once more, 1sc in each st to beg of round, sl st to join.

Fasten off and sew in ends (see page 121).

Round 2: With RS facing, join B at center bottom with a sl stBLO, [ch1, sl stBLO in next st] to beg of round, sl st to join.

Fasten off and sew in ends.

Tree

Using a US size D/3 (3mm) hook and 1 strand of C and 1 strand of D held together, make a magic ring.

Round 1: 4sc into ring. *(4 sts)*

Beg working in BLO.

Round 2: [2sc in next st, 1sc in next st] twice. *(6 sts)*

Round 3: [2sc in next st, 1sc in each of next 2 sts] twice. *(8 sts)*

Round 4: [2sc in next st, 1sc in each of next 3 sts] twice. *(10 sts)*

Round 5: [2sc in next st, 1sc in each of next 4 sts] twice. *(12 sts)*
Round 6: [2sc in next st, 1sc in each of next 5 sts] twice. *(14 sts)*
Round 7: [2sc in next st, 1sc in each of next 6 sts] twice. *(16 sts)*
Round 8: [2sc in next st, 1sc in each of next 7 sts] twice. *(18 sts)*
Round 9: [2sc in next st, 1sc in each of next 8 sts] twice. *(20 sts)*
Round 10: [2sc in next st, 1sc in each of next 9 sts] twice. *(22 sts)*
Round 11: [2sc in next st, 1sc in each of next 10 sts] twice. *(24 sts)*
Round 12: [2sc in next st, 1sc in each of next 11 sts] twice. *(26 sts)*
Round 13: [2sc in next st, 1sc in each of next 12 sts] twice. *(28 sts)*
Round 14: [1sc in each of next 6 sts, 2sc in next st] 4 times. *(32 sts)*
Round 15: [1sc in each of next 7 sts, 2sc in next st] 4 times, sl st to join. *(36 sts)*
Fasten off.
Fold tree flat and push out so that front has a good curve. The flat back will be the part of the tree that is attached to the square.
From now on, work only on curved front part of tree (approx. two thirds of total tree circumference), working from right to left on each row.
Row 16: Using a US steel size 4 (2mm) hook, join F in front loop of Round 15, (2hdcFLO, 1scFLO) in each st around two thirds of tree.
Fasten off.
Row 17: Missing Round 14, join F in front loop of Round 13, (2hdcFLO, 1scFLO) in each st around two thirds of tree.
Fasten off.
Row 18: Missing Round 12, join F in front loop of Round 11, (2hdcFLO, 1scFLO) in each st around two thirds of tree.
Fasten off.
Row 19: Missing Round 10, join F in front loop of Round 9, (2hdcFLO, 1scFLO) in each st around two thirds of tree.
Fasten off.
Row 20: Missing Round 8, join F in front loop of Round 7, (2hdcFLO, 1scFLO) in each st around two thirds of tree.
Fasten off.
Row 21: Missing Round 6, join F in front loop of Round 5, (2hdcFLO, 1scFLO) in each st around two thirds of tree.
Fasten off.
Row 22: Missing Round 4, join F in front loop of Round 3, (2hdcFLO, 1scFLO) in each st around two thirds of tree.
Fasten off.
Row 23: Missing Round 2, join F in front loop of Round 1, 1hdcFLO in each st around two thirds of tree.
Fasten off.
Row 24: Join F in st at top of tree, (1sc, 1hdc, 1sc) in same st.
Fasten off.
Thread yarn ends through to inside or back of tree.

Finishing

Block the square (see page 121).
Decorate the tree with small beads/stars/sequins, either stitching or gluing them in place.
Stick or sew the tree to the square using a needle and thread or hot glue gun. Glue the twig into the base of the tree for the trunk.
Using E work some small French knots (see page 125) on the square for snow, with some across the bottom of the square under the tree.
Add a little glitter glue if desired (optional).

Christmas Wreath Square

This Christmas Wreath square is a beautifully simple make that would be perfect for cards or gift tags. It can be decorated with anything you may have to hand, such as sequins, beads, or even simple French knots in colored wool or thread.

SKILL LEVEL ●

YARN AND MATERIALS

For the background square:

Rowan Handknit Cotton (100% cotton) light worsted (DK) weight yarn, 92yd (85m) per 1¾oz (50g) ball

- 1 ball of Straw shade 381 (yellow) (A)
- Small amount of Raspberry shade 356 (red) (B)

For the wreath:

King Cole Moments (100% polyester) light worsted (DK) weight yarn, 98yd (90m) per 1¾oz (50g) ball

- Small amount of Emerald shade 3228 (green) (C)

Cascade 220 Superwash (100% wool) light worsted (DK) weight yarn, 218yd (200m) per 3½oz (100g) ball

- Small amount of Peridot shade 286 (light green) (D)

Short length of narrow red ribbon

Small bells/beads/stars/sequins

Small amounts of red and white embroidery floss (thread) (optional)

HOOKS AND EQUIPMENT

US size J/10 (6mm) crochet hook

US size E/4 (3.5mm) crochet hook

US size D/3 (3mm) crochet hook

Yarn needle

Blocking mat and pins

Hot glue gun

FINISHED MEASUREMENTS

3¾ x 3¾in (9.5 x 9.5cm)

GAUGE (TENSION)

Exact gauge is not important for this project.

ABBREVIATIONS

See page 127.

Background square

Using a US size E/4 (3.5mm) hook and A, ch17.

Row 1: Starting in second ch from hook, 1sc in back bump of each ch to end, turn. *(16 sts)*

Row 2: Ch1 (does not count as st), 1sc in each st, turn.

Rows 3–18: Rep Row 2.

Fasten off.

EDGING

Round 1: Using a US size D/3 (3mm) hook and A, with RS facing join A at center bottom of square with a sl st, 1sc in same st, *1sc in each st to corner, 3sc in corner st, 1sc in each row-end to next corner, 3sc in corner st; rep from * once more, 1sc in each st to beg of round, sl st to join.

Fasten off and sew in ends (see page 121).

Round 2: With RS facing, join B at center bottom with a sl stBLO, [ch1, sl stBLO in next st] to beg of round, sl st to join.

Fasten off and sew in ends.

Wreath

Using a US size J/10 (6mm) hook and 2 strands of C and 2 strands of D held together, ch23.

Round 1: Starting in second ch from hook, sl st in back bump of each ch to end, sl st in first st to join into a ring. *(22 sts)*

Fasten off and sew in ends.

Trim wreath if needed to neaten it.

Finishing

Block the square (see page 121).

Decorate the wreath with small bells/beads/stars/sequins by either stitching or gluing them into place. Stick the wreath to the square using a hot glue gun. Tie the ribbon into a small bow and attach to the top of the wreath.

Optional: Two candy canes can be stitched at the top corners of the square using small amounts of red and white embroidery floss (thread).

Hanukkah Candelabra Square

This square celebrating Hanukkah could not be simpler to make, because the nine branches of the candelabra are all created with simple crochet chains. Quick and easy to complete, it will shine brightly when on display.

SKILL LEVEL •

YARN AND MATERIALS

For the background square:

Rowan Summerlite (100% cotton), fingering (4-ply) weight yarn, 191yd (175m) per 1¾oz (50g) ball

1 ball of Aqua shade 433 (turquoise) (A)

Small amount of Mustard shade 455 (yellow) (B)

For the candelabra and flames:

Anchor Artiste Metallic (80% viscose, 20% polyester), fingering (4-ply) weight yarn, 109yd (100m) per ⅞oz (25g) ball

Small amount of Gold shade 0300

Cascade Yarns Heritage (75% merino wool, 25% nylon), fingering (4-ply) weight yarn, 437yd (400m) per 3½oz (100g) skein (hank)

Small amounts of:

Golden Yellow shade 5752 (dark yellow)

Royal shade 5615 (blue)

HOOKS AND EQUIPMENT

US size D/3 (3mm) crochet hook

US size B/1-C/2 (2.5mm) crochet hook

US steel size 4 (2mm) hook crochet hook

Yarn needle

Blocking pins and mat

Sewing needle and thread

Pins

FINISHED MEASUREMENTS

3¾ x 3¾in (9.5 x 9.5cm)

GAUGE (TENSION)

Exact gauge is not important for this project.

ABBREVIATIONS

See page 127.

Background square

Using a US size D/3 (3mm) hook and A, ch25.

Row 1: Starting in second ch from hook, 1sc in back bump of each ch to end, turn. *(24 sts)*

Row 2: Ch1 (does not count as st), 1sc in each st, turn.

Rows 3–25: Rep Row 2.

Fasten off.

EDGING

Round 1: Using a US size B/1-C/2 (2.5mm) hook and A, with RS facing join in yarn at center bottom of square with a sl st, 1sc in same st, *1sc in each st to corner, 3sc in corner st, 1sc in each row-end to next corner, 3sc in corner st; rep from * once more, 1sc in each st to beg of round, sl st to join.

Fasten off and sew in ends (see page 121).

Round 2: With RS facing, join B at center bottom with a sl stBLO, *(sl stBLO, ch2, sl stBLO) in next st, sl stBLO in next st; rep from * to beg of round, sl st to join.

Fasten off and sew in ends.

Candelabra arms

Arm 1: Using a US size B/1-C/2 (2.5mm) hook and Gold, ch17. Starting in second ch from hook, sl st in back bump of each ch to end.

Fasten off.

Arm 2: Using a US size B/1-C/2 (2.5mm) hook and Gold, ch27. Starting in second ch from hook, sl st in back bump of each ch to end.

Fasten off.

Arm 3: Using a US size B/1-C/2 (2.5mm) hook and Gold, ch37. Starting in second ch from hook, sl st in back bump of each ch to end.

Fasten off.

Arm 4: Using a US size B/1-C/2 (2.5mm) hook and Gold, ch47. Starting in second ch from hook, sl st in back bump of each ch to end.

Fasten off.

Stem

Using a US size B/1-C/2 (2.5mm) hook and Gold, ch20. Starting in second ch from hook, sl st in each ch to end. Fasten off.

Base

Using a US size B/1-C/2 (2.5mm) hook and Gold, ch7.

Row 1: Starting in second ch from hook, 1sc in each ch to end, turn. *(6 sts)*

Row 2: Ch1 (does not count as st), sc2tog, 1sc in each of next 2 sts, sc2tog. *(4 sts)*

Fasten off.

Using a US steel size 4 (2mm) hook, sl st around edge of base.

Finishing

Block the square (see page 121).

Starting with the longest arm, position and pin the four arms in place, creating the curve, and making sure they are evenly spaced. Stitch in place with a sewing needle and thread. Using a sewing needle and thread, stitch the base and the stem in place, using the photo as a guide.

Using a yarn needle and Golden Yellow, stitch straight stitches (see page 125) to create the nine flames. Use Gold to add a glitter thread to each flame center.

Using Royal, decorate the square with French knots (see page 125).

Decorative Jars

These little bobbly covers turn even the most ordinary of jam jars into the perfect table top decoration for the holidays—whether it's as a tea light holder, a sweet jar, or even a vase for small posies. For that additional finish, each jar can be personalized with a tag to make it extra special.

SKILL LEVEL ●●

YARN AND MATERIALS

Rowan Creative Linen (50% linen, 50% cotton) light worsted (DK) weight yarn, approx. 218yd (200m) per 3½oz (100g) ball

1 ball each of shades:

Cloud 0620 (A)

Natural 0621 (B)

3¼in (8cm) tall screw-top round glass jar

5¼in (13cm) tall screw-top round glass jar

Ribbon

Luggage/parcel tag

HOOKS AND EQUIPMENT

US size C/2-D/3 (3mm) crochet hook

Stitch marker

Yarn needle

FINISHED MEASUREMENTS

Small jar: 3¼in (8cm) tall, 3in (7.5cm) diameter at top

Tall jar: 5¼in (13cm) tall, 3in (7.5cm) diameter at top

GAUGE (TENSION)

15 sts x 15 rows = 3¼ x 3in (8 x 7.5cm) working single crochet, using a US size C/2-D/3 (3mm) crochet hook.

ABBREVIATIONS

See page 127.

SPECIAL ABBREVIATIONS

MB (make bobble): *yoh, insert hook in st, yoh and pull through st, yoh, pull yarn through 2 loops on hook; rep from * 3 more times in same st, yoh, pull through all 5 loops on hook.

For the jar cover

BASE

Round 1: Using A or B, make a magic ring, 8sc into the ring.

Work in a continuous spiral. PM in last st and move up as each round is finished.

Round 2: 2sc in each st to end. *(16 sts)*

Round 3: *1sc, 2sc in next st; rep from * to end. *(24 sts)*

Round 4: *1sc in each of first 2 sts, 2sc in next st; rep from * to end. *(32 sts)*

Round 5: *1sc in each of first 3 sts, 2sc in next st; rep from * to end. *(40 sts)*

Round 6: 1sc in each st to end.

Round 7: *1sc in each of first 4 sts, 2sc in next st; rep from * to end. *(48 sts)*

Round 8: *1sc in each of first 5 sts, 2sc in next st; rep from * to end. *(56 sts)*

Round 9: 1sc in each st to end, join with a sl st in first st.

Round 10: Ch1, 1sc BLO in each st to end, join with a sl st in first st.

Begin the sides:

Round 11: Ch1, 1sc in each st to end, join with a sl st in first st.

Round 12: Ch1, 1sc in each st to end, join with a sl st in first st.

Round 13 (bobble row 1): Join in A or B contrast color but work over it in main color. Using main color, ch1, 1sc in each of first 2 sts, *MB using contrast color, working final yoh of bobble using main color, 1sc in each of next 5 sts; rep from * to end, join with a sl st in first st, leave contrast color hanging loose at back ready for next bobble round.

Rounds 14 and 15: Ch1, 1sc in each st to end, join with a sl st in first st. *(56 sts)*

Round 16 (bobble row 2): Join in contrast color but work over it in main color. Using main color, ch1, 1sc in each of first 6 sts, *MB using contrast color,

TIPS

To create a neat joining seam at the back of the jar where each round joins, sl st at the end of each round, make 1 chain and work the first single crochet of the next round into the same stitch as the chain 1. Use a stitch marker to mark the chain at the beginning of the round to help you keep track.

When working bobbles in coordinating colors, join in the bobble yarn at the beginning of each bobble row. As you work, lay this yarn color along the top of the last row of stitches so that it gets worked in as you crochet along the row. When you are ready to make a bobble, bring the bobble color up from behind your work and work the bobble. To finish the bobble, work the final yarn over hook in the main color, laying the bobble color back along the top of the last row again to keep it worked in. At the end of the row fasten off the bobble yarn, leaving an end long enough to sew in.

Merry Christmas

working final yoh of bobble using main color, 1sc in each of next 5 sts; rep from * to last 2 sts, MB using contrast color, working final yoh of bobble using main color, 1sc in last st with main color, join with a sl st in first st, leave contrast color hanging loose at back ready for next bobble round.

Rounds 17 and 18: Ch1, 1sc in each st to end, join with a sl st in first st. *(56 sts)*

Round 19 (bobble row 3): Join in contrast color but work over it in main color. Using main color, ch1, 1sc in each of first 3 sts, *MB using contrast color, working final yoh of bobble using main color, 1sc in each of next 5 sts; rep from * to end, ending last rep with 1sc in each of last 4 sts, join with a sl st in first st, leave contrast color hanging loose at back ready for next bobble round.

Rounds 20 and 21: Ch1, 1sc in each st to end, join with a sl st in first st. 56 sts.

Round 22 (bobble row 4): Join in contrast color but work over it in main color. Using main color, ch1, 1sc in first st, *MB in next st using contrast color, working final yoh of bobble using main color, 1sc in each of next 5 sts; rep from * to last 7 sts, MB in next st using contrast color, working final yoh of bobble using main color, 1sc in main color in each of last 6 sts, join with a sl st in first st.

Small jar only:

Fasten off contrast color.

Tall jar only:

Rep rounds 11–19, fastening off contrast color at end of round 19.

Both jars:

Next round: Ch1, 1sc in each st to end, join with a sl st in first st. *(56 sts)*

Next round: Ch1, *1sc in each of first 4 sts, sc2tog; rep from * to last 2 sts, 1sc in each of last 2 sts, join with a sl st in first st. *(47 sts)*

Next round: Ch1, *1sc in each of first 3 sts, sc2tog; rep from * to last 2 sts, 1sc in each of last 2 sts, join with a sl st in first st. *(38 sts)*

Next 2 rounds: Ch1, 1sc in each st to end, join with a sl st in first st.

Fasten off.

Next round: Re-join contrast color, ch2 (does not count as st), 1hdc in each st to end, join with a sl st in first st.

Border round: [Sl st, ch2, sl st] to end, join with a sl st in first st. Fasten off.

Making up and finishing

Slip the cover onto the jar and add the finishing ribbon and personalized tags.

MAKE IT YOURS

This cover can be adapted to any size straight-sided jar simply by making the base of the cover the same size as the base of your jar—but for the pattern to work, the stitch count when you begin the sides should be a multiple of 6 + 2. Once you have the correct base size, the following rounds for the sides should fit perfectly—although the final stitch counts will vary.

Mailbox and Presents Square

A bright red mailbox, a pile of presents, and snow—a square to get you in the mood for all things Christmas! Whether made as one square for some bunting, a gift tag, or a card, this little festive crochet square is very quick and simple to make.

Background square

Using a US size D/3 (3mm) hook and A, ch23.

Row 1: Starting in second ch from hook, 1sc in back bump of each ch to end, turn. *(22 sts)*

Row 2: Ch1 (does not count as st), 1sc in each st, turn.

Rows 3–22: Rep Row 2.

Fasten off.

EDGING

Round 1: Using a US size B/1–C/2 (2.5mm) hook and A, with RS facing join in yarn at center bottom of square with a sl st, 1sc in same st, *1sc in each st to corner, 3sc in corner st, 1sc in each row-end to next corner, 3sc in corner st; rep from * once more, 1sc in each st to beg of round, sl st to join.

Fasten off and sew in ends (see page 121).

Round 2: With RS facing, join B at center bottom with a sl stBLO, *sl stBLO in each of next 2 sts, ch3; rep from * to beg of round, sl st to join.

Fasten off and sew in ends.

Mailbox

Using a US size B/1–C/2 (2.5mm) hook and Forged Iron, ch12.

Row 1: Starting in second ch from hook, 1sc in back bump of each ch to end, turn. *(11 sts)*

Rows 2 and 3: Ch1 (does not count as st throughout), 1sc in each st, turn.

Row 4: Ch1, sc2tog, 1sc in each of next 7 sts, sc2tog, turn. *(9 sts)*

Fasten off.

Row 5: Join Red at beg of Row 4 with a sl stBLO, 1scBLO in same st, 1scBLO in each st, turn. *(9 sts)*

SKILL LEVEL •

YARN AND MATERIALS

For the background square:

Rowan Summerlite (100% cotton), fingering (4-ply) weight yarn, 191yd (175m) per 1¾oz (50g) ball

1 ball of Aqua shade 433 (turquoise) (A)

Cascade Yarns Ultra Pima (100% cotton) light worsted (DK) weight yarn, 220yd (200m) per 3½oz (100g) skein (hank)

Small amount of Lipstick Red shade 3755 (B)

For the mailbox and presents:

Cascade Yarns Heritage (75% merino wool, 25% nylon), fingering (4-ply) weight yarn, 437yd (400m) per 3½oz (100g) skein (hank)

Small amounts of:

Forged Iron shade 5736 (dark gray)

Red shade 5607

Limestone shade 5681 (beige)

White shade 5682

Anchor Artiste Metallic (20% polyester, 80% viscose), fingering (4-ply) weight yarn, 109yd (100m) per ⅞oz (25g) ball

Small amount of Gold shade 300

Small piece of cardboard

HOOKS AND EQUIPMENT

US size D/3 (3mm) crochet hook

US size B/1–C/2 (2.5mm) crochet hook

US steel size 4 (2mm) crochet hook

Yarn needle

Blocking pins and mat

Sewing needle and thread

Scissors for cardboard

FINISHED MEASUREMENTS

4 x 4in (10 x 10cm)

GAUGE (TENSION)

Exact gauge is not important for this project.

ABBREVIATIONS

See page 127.

Rows 6–17: Ch1, 1sc in each st, turn.
Row 18: Ch3, starting in second ch from hook, 1sc in each of next 2 ch, 1sc in each of next 9 sts, turn. *(11 sts)*
Row 19: Ch3, starting in second ch from hook, 1sc in each of next 2 ch, 1sc in each of next 9 sts, leave rem sts unworked, turn.
Row 20: Ch1, sc2tog, 1sc in each of next 5 sts, sc2tog, leave rem sts unworked, turn. *(7 sts)*
Row 21: Ch1, sl st in next st, 1sc in next st, 1hdc in each of next 3 sts, 1sc in next st, sl st in last st.
Fasten off.

EDGING
Using US steel size 4 (2mm) hook and Red or Forged Iron as colors dictate, 1sc in each st or row-end around mailbox, working 2sc in 1 st or row-end where needed to keep shape.

BASE TOP EDGING
Using US steel size 4 (2mm) hook and Forged Iron, work a line of sl st surface crochet along top edge of base of mailbox.
Fasten off.

TOP EDGING
Using US steel size 4 (2mm) hook and Red, work a line of sl st surface crochet along Row 17 of mailbox.
Fasten off and sew in ends.

Large present
Using US steel size 4 (2mm) hook and Red, ch10.
Row 1: Starting in second ch from hook, 1sc in back bump of each ch to end, turn. *(9 sts)*
Rows 2–6: Ch1 (does not count as st), 1sc in each st, turn.
Fasten off.

EDGING
Round 1: Join Red in top right corner, *1sc in each st to corner, (1sc, ch2, 1sc) in corner st, 1sc in each row-end to next corner, (1sc, ch2, 1sc) in corner st; rep from * once more, sl st to join.
Fasten off and sew in ends.

Small present
Using US steel size 4 (2mm) hook and Limestone, ch7.
Row 1: Starting in second ch from hook, 1sc in back bump of each ch to end, turn. *(6 sts)*
Rows 2–4: Ch1 (does not count as st), 1sc in each st, turn.
Fasten off.

EDGING
Round 1: Join Limestone in top right corner, *1sc in each st to corner, (1sc, ch2, 1sc) in corner st, 1sc in each row-end to next corner, (1sc, ch2, 1sc) in corner st; rep from * once more, sl st to join.
Fasten off and sew in ends.

Finishing
Block the square (see page 121).
Thread Forged Iron into a yarn needle and stitch the opening of the mailbox with long straight stitches (see page 125). Using Gold and a sewing needle stitch a crown shape on the mailbox, and then work a French knot (see page 125) in Gold for the very top of the mailbox. Using White in a yarn needle, sew two white squares onto the mailbox following the photo as a guide.
Using Limestone in a sewing needle stitch French knots for dots on the large present. Tie a length of Limestone around the present, attaching to secure on the reverse. Tie a length of Red around the small present, attaching to secure on the reverse.
Using a sewing needle and thread, stitch the outside edge of the mailbox to the square, creating a 3-D effect to the mailbox as you sew. Leave the bottom edge open.
Cut out a small rectangle of card the same width as the mailbox, roughly shape into a curve, and carefully insert this into the mailbox through the opening at the base to form a solid shape.
Using a sewing needle and thread, stitch the presents to the square. Using Red, tie a bow and sew to the top of the small present.
Using White in a yarn needle, work French knots over the background and along the bottom of the square for snow.

Diwali Candle Square

While this little diya lamp is made out of yarn rather than clay, it will still shine brightly during Diwali. Bright colors and gold yarn add to the celebratory feel of this square, whether sent as a greetings card or framed in a small box picture frame.

SKILL LEVEL ●

YARN AND MATERIALS

For the background square:

Rowan Summerlite (100% cotton), fingering (4-ply) weight yarn, 191yd (175m) per 1¾oz (50g) ball

- 1 ball of Aqua shade 433 (turquoise) (A)
- Small amount of Mustard shade 455 (yellow) (B)

For the Diya lamp and flame:

Cascade Yarns Heritage (75% merino wool, 25% nylon), fingering (4-ply) weight yarn, 437yd (400m) per 3½oz (100g) skein (hank)

- Small amounts of:
- Tutu shade 5613 (pink)
- Golden Yellow shade 5752 (dark yellow)
- Herb shade 5658 (green)
- Royal shade 5615 (blue)

Anchor Artiste Metallic (20% polyester, 80% viscose), fingering (4-ply) weight yarn, 109yd (100m) per ⅞oz (25g) ball

- Small amount of Gold shade 0300

Small beads/sequins/stars

HOOKS AND EQUIPMENT

US size D/3 (3mm) crochet hook

US size B/1-C/2 (2.5mm) crochet hook

US steel size 4 (2mm) crochet hook

Yarn needle

Blocking pins and mat

Sewing needle and thread

FINISHED MEASUREMENTS

3¾ x 3¾in (9.5 x 9.5cm)

GAUGE (TENSION)

Exact gauge is not important for this project.

ABBREVIATIONS

See page 127.

Background square

Using a US size D/3 (3mm) hook and A, ch25.

Row 1: Starting in second ch from hook, 1sc in back bump of each ch to end, turn. *(24 sts)*

Row 2: Ch1 (does not count as st), 1sc in each st, turn.

Rows 3–25: Rep Row 2.

Fasten off.

EDGING

Round 1: Using a US size B/1–C/2 (2.5mm) hook and A, with RS facing join in yarn at center bottom of square with a sl st, 1sc in same st, *1sc in each st to corner, 3sc in corner st, 1sc in each row-end to next corner, 3sc in corner st; rep from * once more, 1sc in each st to beg of round, sl st to join.

Fasten off and sew in ends (see page 121).

Round 2: With RS facing, join B at center bottom with a sl stBLO, *(sl stBLO, ch2, sl stBLO) in next st, sl stBLO in next st; rep from * to beg of round, sl st to join.

Fasten off and sew in ends.

Diya lamp

Using a US size B/1–C/2 (2.5mm) hook and 2 strands of Tutu held together, make a magic ring.

Round 1: 4sc into ring. *(4 sts)*

Round 2: 2sc in each st. *(8 sts)*

Round 3: 2sc in each st. *(16 sts)*

Round 4: [1sc in next st, 2sc in next st] 8 times. *(24 sts)*

Round 5: 1sc in each st.

Round 6: [1sc in each of next 2 sts, 1hdc in each of next 2 sts, 1dc in each of next 4 sts, 1hdc in each of next 2 sts , 1sc in each of next 2 sts] twice, sl st to join.

Fasten off.

Round 7: Join in 2 strands of Golden Yellow held together, [1scBLO in each of next 5 sts, 2scBLO in next st] 4 times, sl st to join. *(28 sts)*

Fasten off.

Round 8: Join in 2 strands of Herb held together, [1scBLO in each of next 3 sts, 2scBLO in next st] 7 times, sl st to join. *(35 sts)*

Fasten off.

Round 9: Join in 2 strands of Royal held together, [1scBLO in each of next 4 sts, 2scBLO in next st] 4 times, 1hdcBLO in next st, 1trBLO in next st, ch2, sl stBLO in second ch from hook, 1trBLO in next st, 1hdcBLO in next st, 2scBLO in next st, [1scBLO in each of next 4 sts, 2scBLO in next st] twice, sl st to join.

Fasten off and sew in ends.

Flame

Using a US steel size 4 (2mm) hook and 2 strands of Golden Yellow held together, make a magic ring.

Round 1: 4sc into ring. *(4 sts)*

Round 2: [1sc in next st, 2sc in next st] twice. *(6 sts)*

Round 3: 1sc in each st.

Round 4: [1sc in each of next 2 sts, 2sc in next st] twice. *(8 sts)*

Round 5: 1sc in each st.

Round 6: [1sc in each of next 2 sts, sc2tog] twice. *(6 sts)*

Use yarn tail to close up top of flame to a point.

Finishing

Block the square (see page 121).

Using a yarn needle and either the colored yarns or Gold, decorate the lamp with small running stitches and French knots (see page 125). Add Gold straight stitches from the base of the flame to the tip.

Fold the back of the lamp in toward the center to create a flat back and a curved front. Stitch the lamp to the square, keeping the curved 3-D effect as you sew.

Decorate the rest of the square with beads/stars/sequins and French knots.

Techniques

This section guides you through all the crochet and finishing techniques that you will need to make the squares and projects in this book.

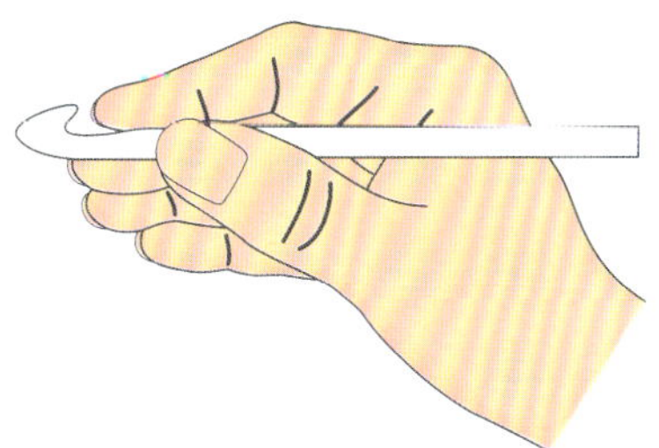

Holding the hook

Pick up your hook as though you are picking up a pen or pencil. Keeping the hook held loosely between your fingers and thumb, turn your hand so that the palm is facing up and the hook is balanced in your hand and resting in the space between your index finger and your thumb.

You can also hold the hook like a knife—this may be easier if you are working with a large hook or with bulky (chunky) yarn. Choose the method that you find most comfortable.

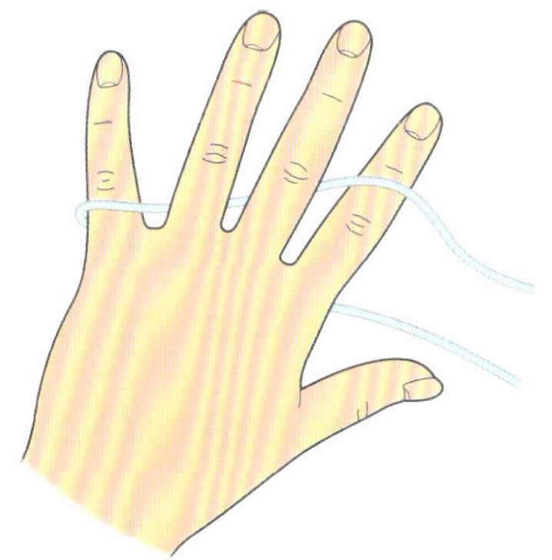

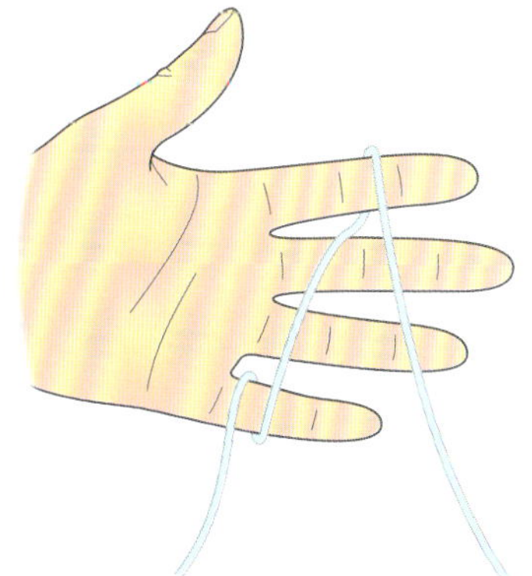

Holding the yarn

1 Pick up the yarn with your little finger in the opposite hand to your hook, with your palm facing upward and with the short end in front. Turn your hand to face downward, with the yarn on top of your index finger and under the other two fingers and wrapped right around the little finger, as shown above.

2 Turn your hand to face you, ready to hold the work in your middle finger and thumb. Keeping your index finger only at a slight curve, hold the work or the slip knot using the same hand, between your middle finger and your thumb and just below the crochet hook and loop(s) on the hook.

Holding the hook and yarn while crocheting

Keep your index finger, with the yarn draped over it, at a slight curve, and hold your work (or the slip knot) using the same hand, between your middle finger and your thumb and just below the crochet hook and loop(s) on the hook.

As you draw the loop through the hook, release the yarn on the index finger to allow the loop to stay loose on the hook. If you tense your index finger, the yarn will become too tight and pull the loop on the hook too tight for you to draw the yarn through.

HOLDING THE HOOK AND YARN FOR LEFT-HANDERS

Some left-handers learn to crochet like right-handers, but others learn with everything reversed—with the hook in the left hand and the yarn in the right.

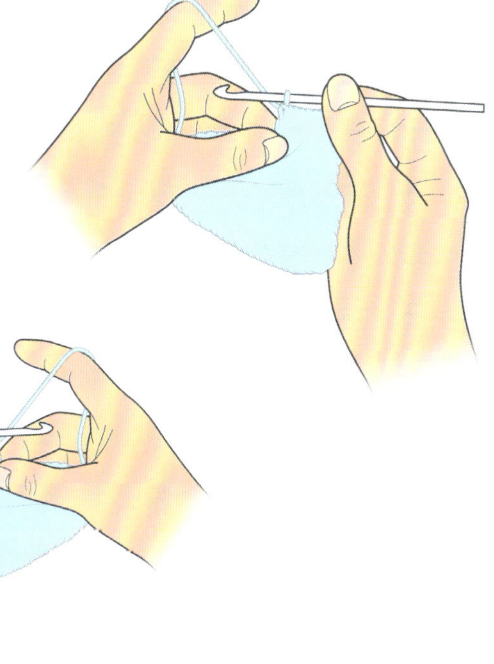

Making a slip knot

The simplest way is to make a circle with the yarn, so that the loop is facing downward.

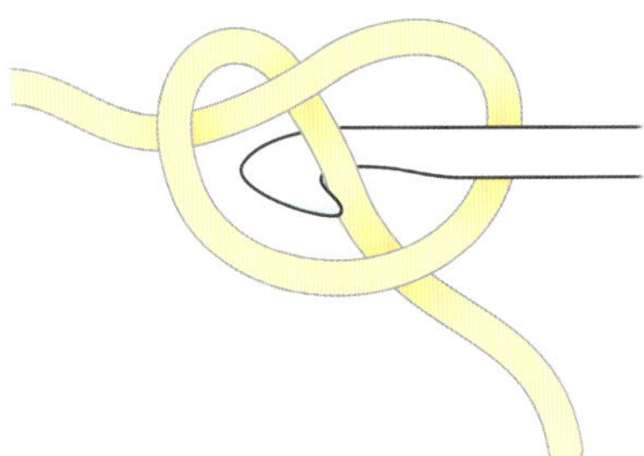

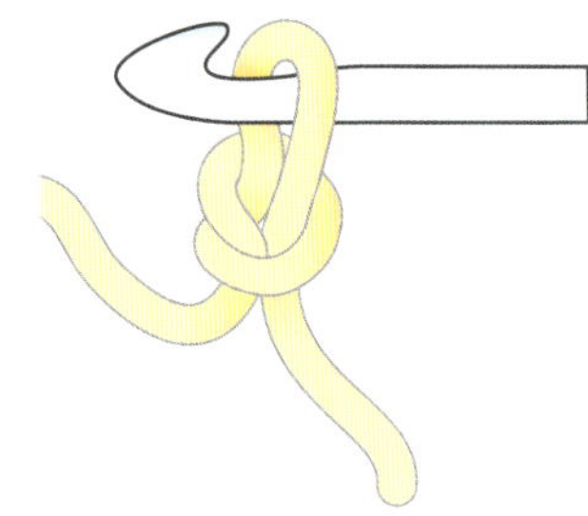

1 In one hand, hold the circle at the top where the yarn crosses, and let the tail drop down at the back so that it falls across the center of the loop. With your free hand or the tip of a crochet hook, pull a loop through the circle.

2 Put the hook into the loop and pull gently so that it forms a loose loop on the hook.

Yarn over hook (yoh)

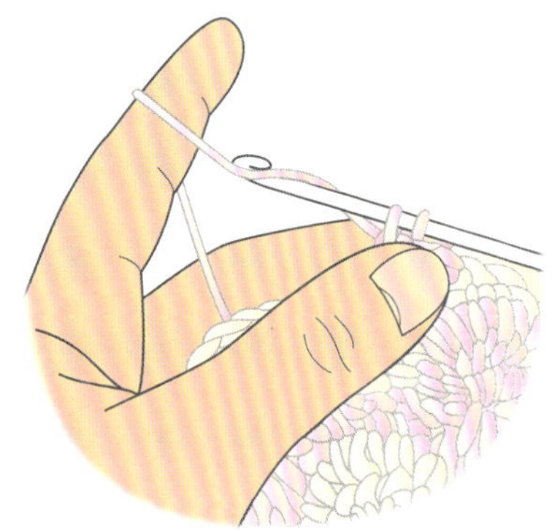

To create a stitch, catch the yarn from behind with the hook pointing upward. As you gently pull the yarn through the loop on the hook, turn the hook so it faces downward and slide the yarn through the loop. The loop on the hook should be kept loose enough for the hook to slide through easily.

Chain (ch)

1 Using the hook, wrap the yarn round the hook ready to pull it through the loop on the hook.

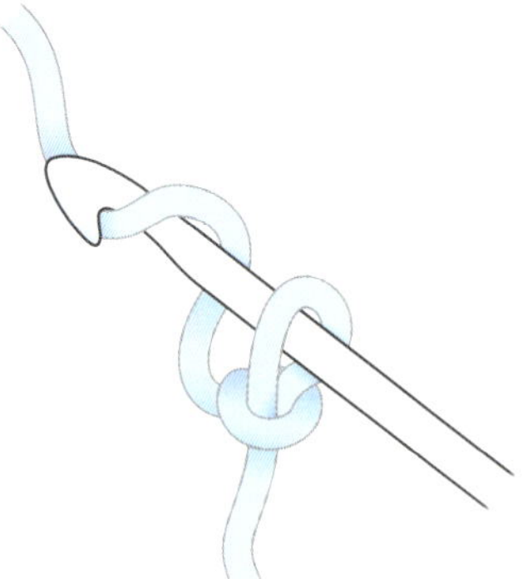

2 Pull through, creating a new loop on the hook. Continue in this way to create a chain of the required length.

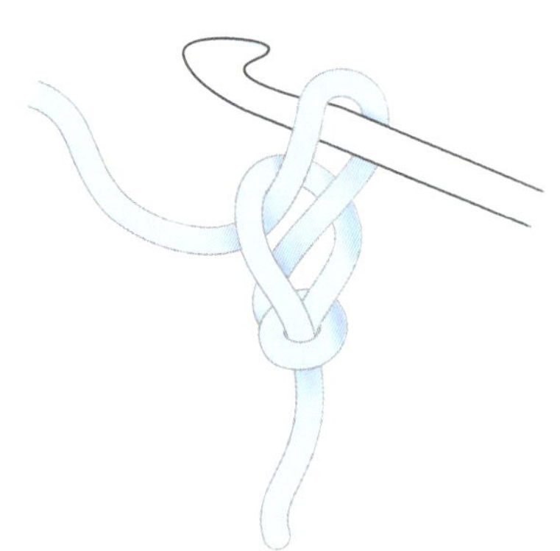

Working into a foundation chain

WORKING INTO THE FRONT OF THE FOUNDATION CHAIN

The front of the chain (the right side) is the smooth side: each chain makes a little "V", as shown here. To make the first stitch into your foundation chain, using the point of the tip of the hook and with the hook tilted slightly sideways, insert the hook into the middle of the chain, picking up the loop at the top of the chain.

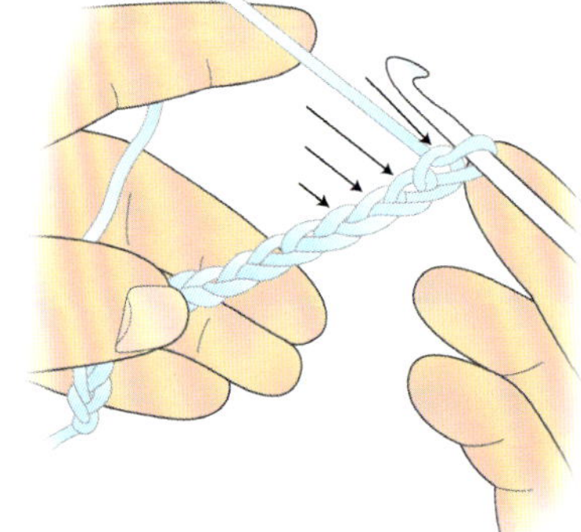

WORKING INTO THE BACK OF THE FOUNDATION CHAIN

The back of the chain (the wrong side) is more bumpy, with little ridges. To make the first stitch into the back of the foundation chain, using the point of the tip of the hook and with the hook tilted slightly sideways, insert the hook into the bump at the back of the chain.

Chain ring

If you are crocheting a round shape, one way of starting off is by crocheting a number of chains following the instructions in your pattern, and then joining them into a circle.

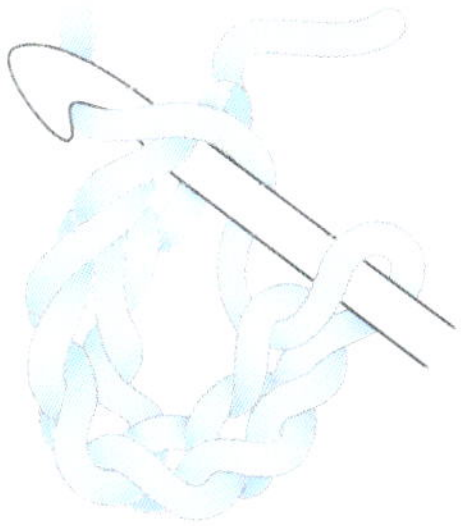

1 To join the chain into a circle, insert the crochet hook into the first chain that you made (not into the slip knot), yarn over hook.

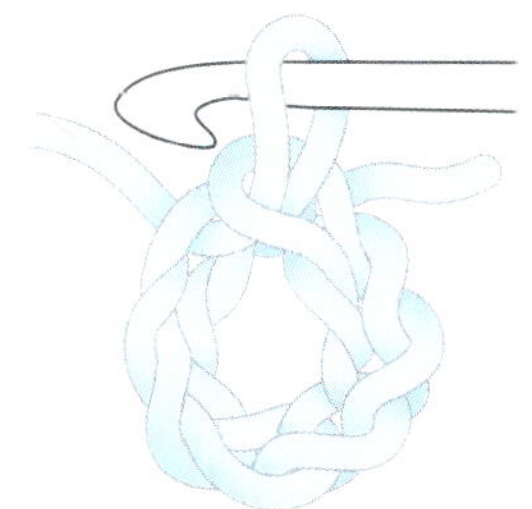

2 Pull the yarn through the chain and through the loop on your hook at the same time, thereby creating a slip stitch and forming a circle. You now have a chain ring ready to work stitches into as instructed in the pattern.

Magic ring

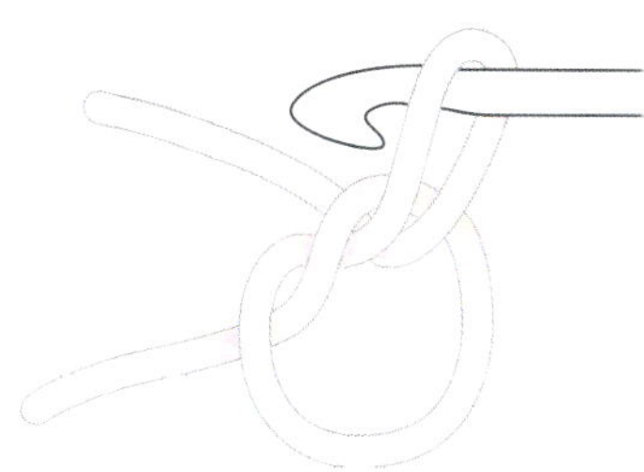

This is a useful starting technique if you do not want a visible hole in the center of your round. Loop the yarn around your finger, insert the hook through the ring, yarn over hook, pull through the ring to make the first chain. Work the number of stitches required into the ring and then pull the end to tighten the center ring and close the hole.

Making rows

When making straight rows, you turn the work at the end of each row and make a turning chain to create the height you need for the stitch you are working with, as for making rounds.

Single crochet = 1 chain
Half double crochet = 2 chains
Double crochet = 3 chains
Treble = 4 chains

Making rounds

When working in rounds, the work is not turned, so you are always working from one side. Depending on the pattern you are working, a "round" can be square. Start each round by making one or more chains to create the height you need for the stitch you are working:

Single crochet = 1 chain
Half double crochet = 2 chains
Double crochet = 3 chains
Treble = 4 chains

Work the required stitches to complete the round. At the end of the round, slip stitch into the top of the chain to close the round.

Continuous spiral

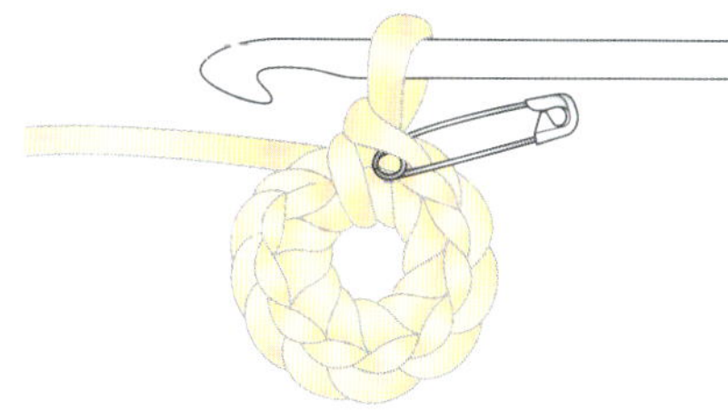

If you work in a spiral you do not need a turning chain. After completing the base ring, place a stitch marker in the first stitch and then continue to crochet around. When you have made a round and reached the point where the stitch marker is, work this stitch, take out the stitch marker from the previous round and put it back into the first stitch of the new round. A safety pin or piece of yarn in a contrasting color makes a good stitch marker.

Slip stitch (sl st)

A slip stitch doesn't create any height and is often used as the last stitch to create a smooth and even round or row.

1 To make a slip stitch: first put the hook through the work, yarn over hook.

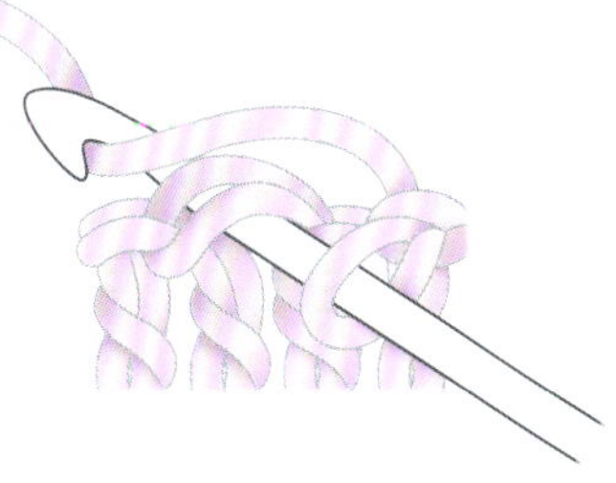

2 Pull the yarn through both the work and through the loop on the hook at the same time, so you will have 1 loop on the hook.

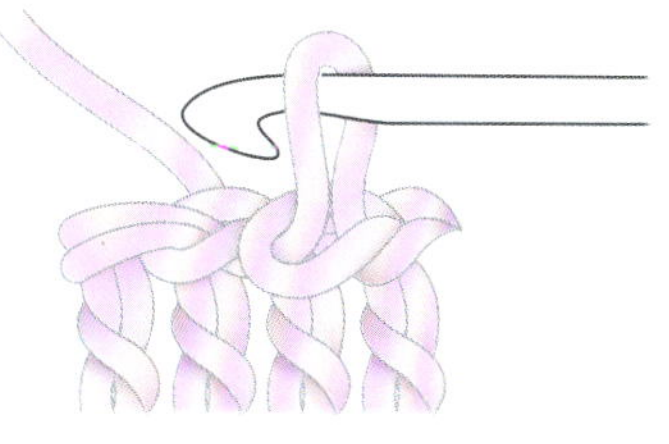

Working into top of stitch

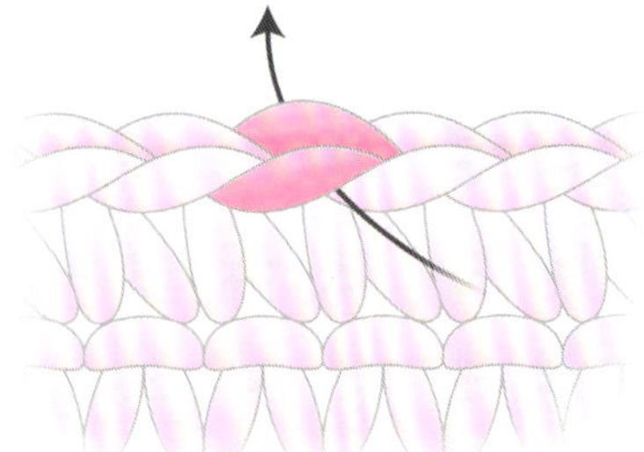

Unless otherwise directed, always insert the hook under both of the two loops on top of the stitch—this is the standard technique.

Working into front loop of stitch (FLO)

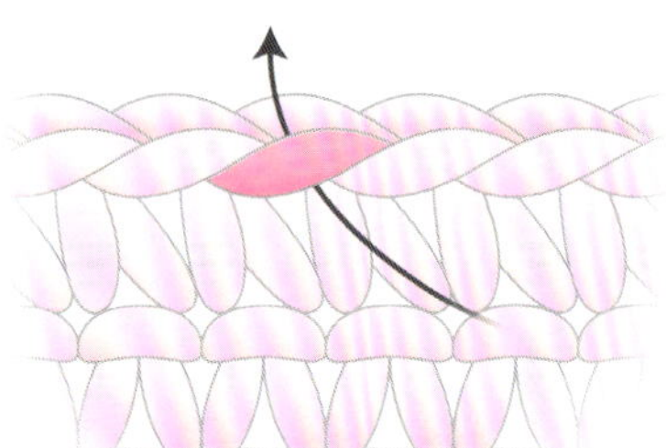

To work into the front loop of a stitch, pick up the front loop from underneath at the front of the work.

Working into back loop of stitch (BLO)

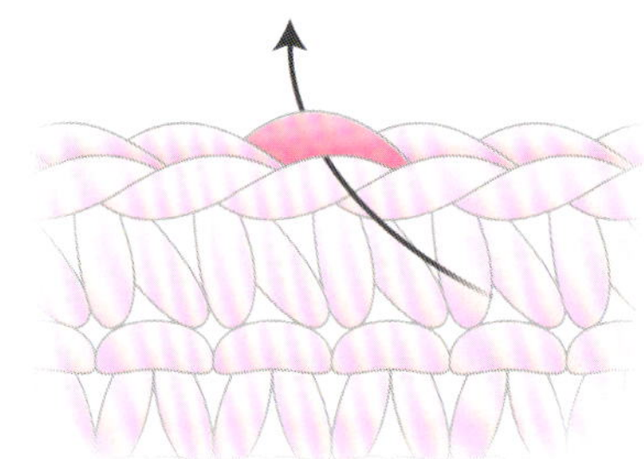

To work into the back loop of the stitch, insert the hook between the front and the back loop, picking up the back loop from the front of the work.

Single crochet (sc)

1 Insert the hook into your work, yarn over hook and pull the yarn through the work only. You will then have 2 loops on the hook.

2 Yarn over hook again and pull through the 2 loops on the hook. You will then have 1 loop on the hook.

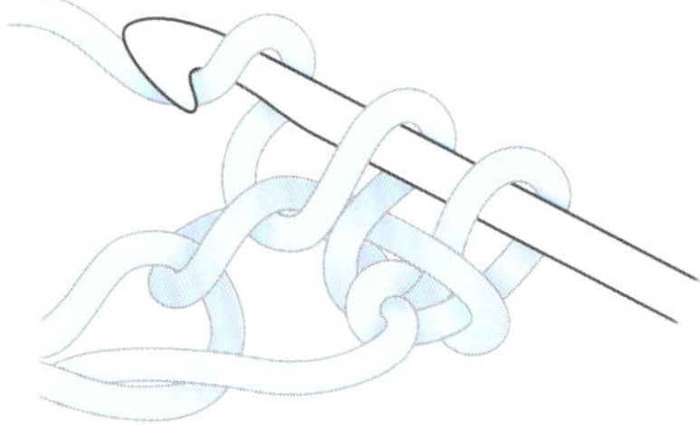

Half double crochet (hdc)

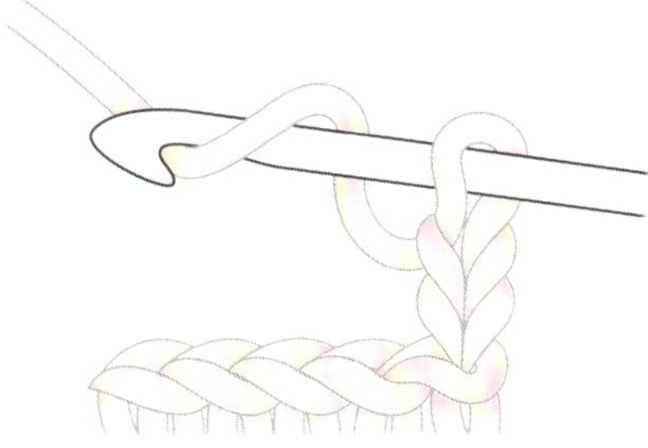

1 Before inserting the hook into the work, wrap the yarn round the hook and put the hook through the work with the yarn wrapped around.

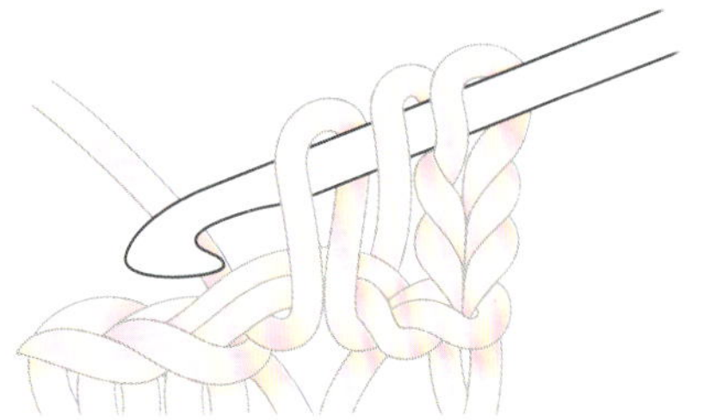

2 Yarn over hook again and pull through the first loop on the hook.
You now have 3 loops on the hook.

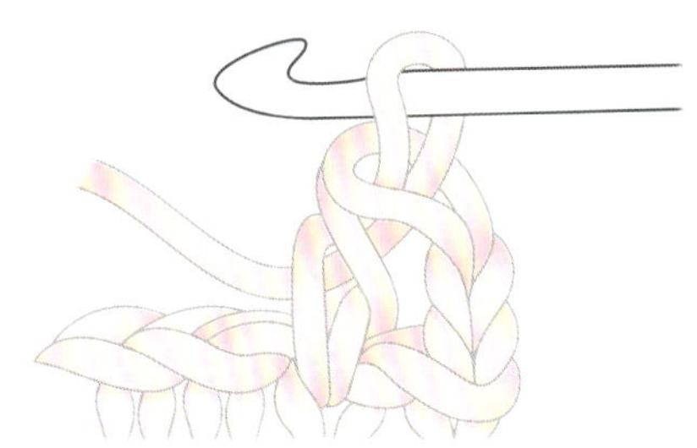

3 Yarn over hook and pull the yarn through all 3 loops. You will be left with 1 loop on the hook.

Double crochet (dc)

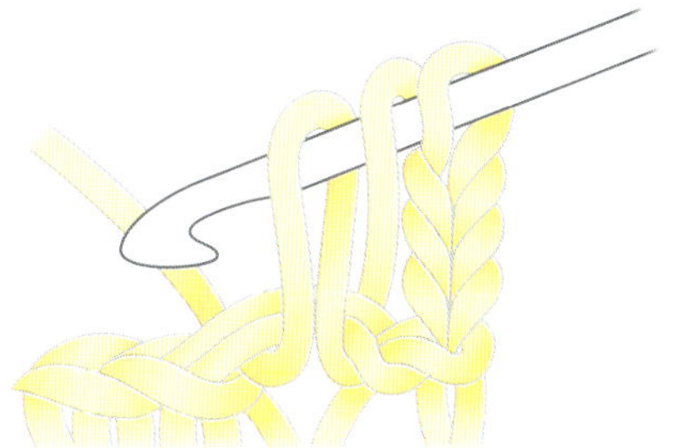

1 Before inserting the hook into the work, wrap the yarn over the hook. Put the hook through the work with the yarn wrapped around, yarn over hook again and pull through the first loop on the hook. You now have 3 loops on the hook.

2 Yarn over hook again, pull the yarn through the first 2 loops on the hook. You now have 2 loops on the hook.

3 Pull the yarn through 2 loops again. You will be left with 1 loop on the hook.

Treble crochet (tr)

Yarn over hook twice, insert the hook into the stitch, yarn over hook, pull a loop through (4 loops on hook), yarn over hook, pull the yarn through 2 stitches (3 loops on hook), yarn over hook, pull a loop through the next 2 stitches (2 loops on hook), yarn over hook, pull a loop through the last 2 stitches. You will be left with 1 loop on the hook.

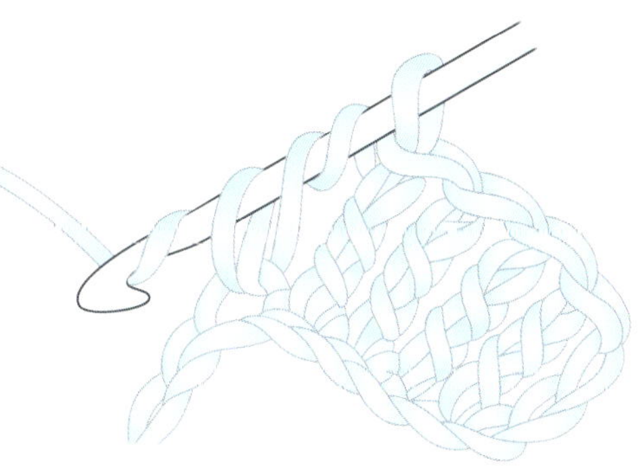

Increasing

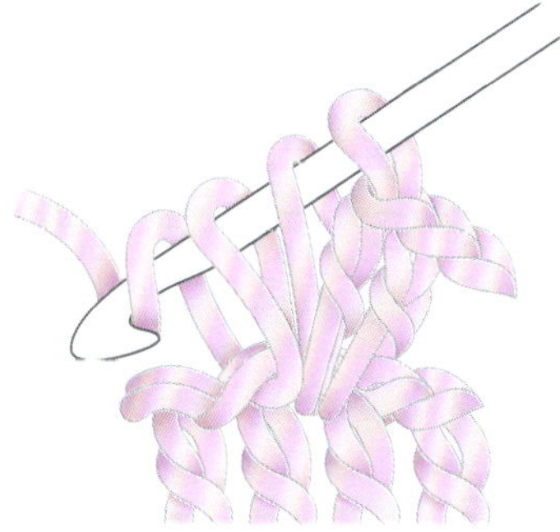

Make two or three stitches into one stitch or space from the previous row. The illustration shows a double crochet increase being made.

Decreasing

You can decrease by either missing the next stitch and continuing to crochet, or by crocheting two or more stitches together. The basic technique for crocheting stitches together is the same, no matter which stitch you are using. The following example shows sc2tog.

SINGLE CROCHET TWO STITCHES TOGETHER (SC2TOG)

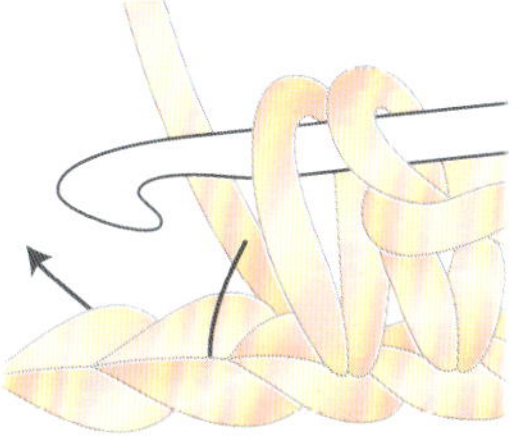

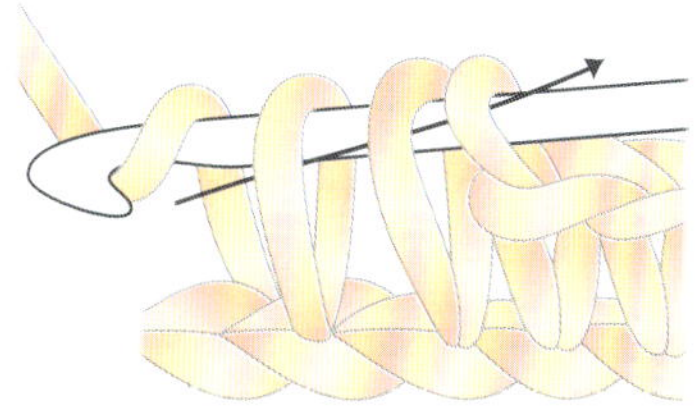

1 Insert the hook into your work, yarn over hook and pull the yarn through the work (2 loops on hook). Insert the hook in next stitch, yarn over hook, and pull the yarn through.

2 Yarn over hook again and pull through all 3 loops on the hook. You will then have 1 loop on the hook.

Enclosing a yarn tail

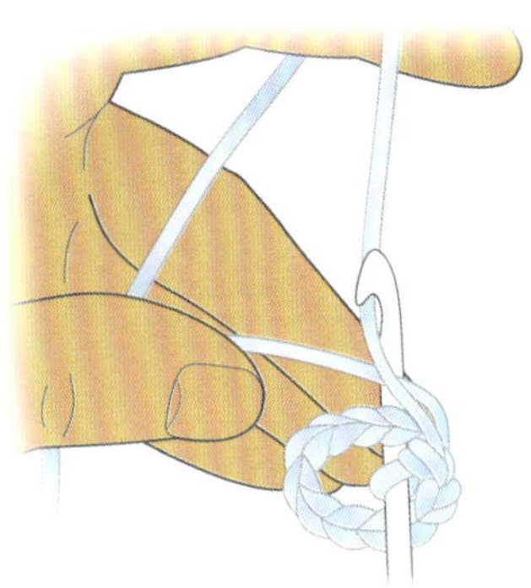

You may find that the yarn tail gets in the way as you work; you can enclose this into the stitches as you go by placing the tail at the back as you wrap the yarn. This also saves having to sew this tail end in later.

Joining yarn with a slip stitch

You can use this technique when changing color, or when joining in a new ball of yarn as one runs out.

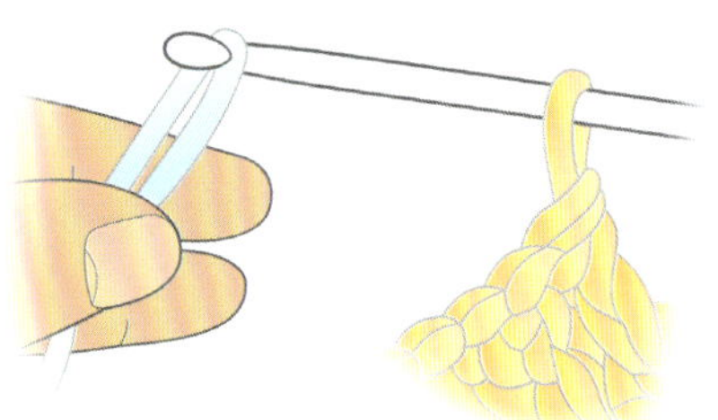

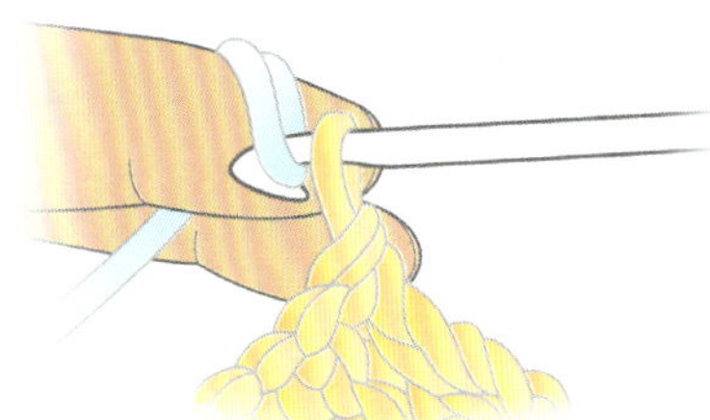

1 Keep the loop of the old yarn on the hook. Drop the tail and catch a loop of the strand of the new yarn with the crochet hook.

2 Draw the new yarn through the loop on the hook, keeping the old loop drawn tight and continue as instructed in the pattern.

Changing color in the middle of a row or round or on last yarn over hook

This method can be used to create a neat color join in the middle of a row or round, or on the last yarn over hook (yoh).

JOINING A NEW COLOR INTO SINGLE CROCHET

1 Make a single crochet stitch (see page 118), but do not draw the final loop through, so there are 2 loops on the hook. Drop the old yarn, catch the new yarn with the hook and draw it through both loops to complete the stitch and join in the new color at the same time.

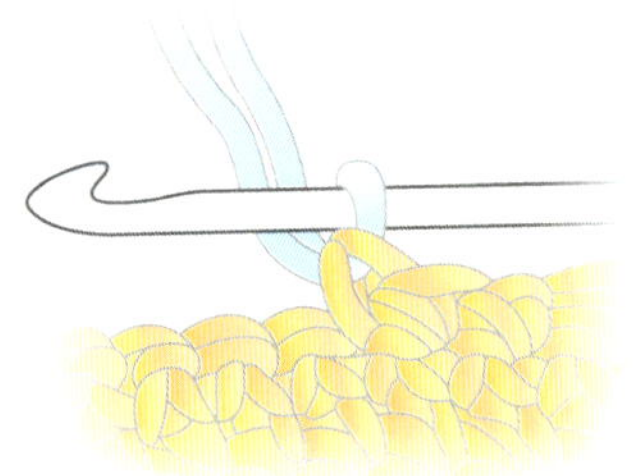

2 Continue to crochet with the new yarn. Cut the old yarn leaving a 6in (15cm) tail and weave the tail in (see right) after working a row, or once the work is complete.

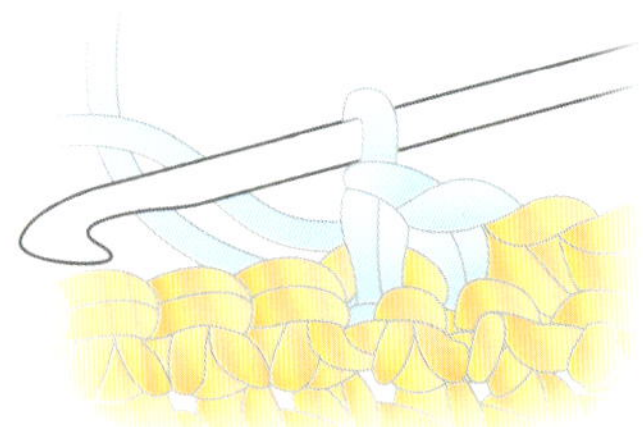

Working over yarn along a row

Working over the yarn along a row involves carrying one or more additional colors through the work until you are ready to use them. It's the crochet equivalent of Fair Isle or stranding in knitting, but with the bonus that the second color is not visible at the back of the work—it is fully enclosed in the stitches of the first color.

JOINING A NEW COLOR INTO SINGLE CROCHET

1 Hold the second color yarn along the top of the stitches from the previous row. You can do this from the beginning of a row, or join it a few stitches before you need to start using it, if it is only going to be used for a small area.

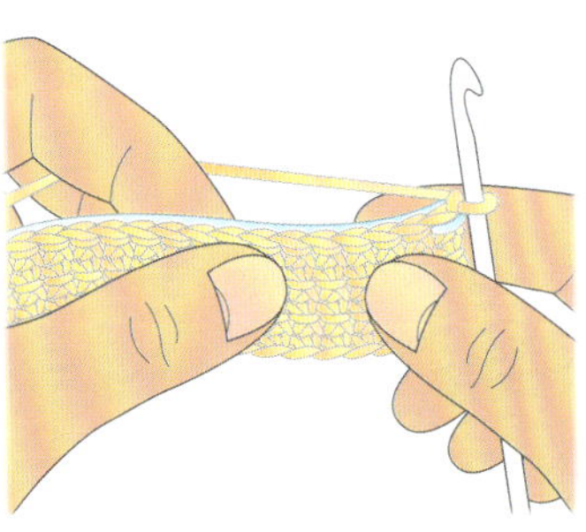

2 Work stitches in the normal way in the first color, but going over the second color and ensuring it is "trapped" within the stitches. Continue working in this way, carrying the second color until you are ready to work a stitch in it.

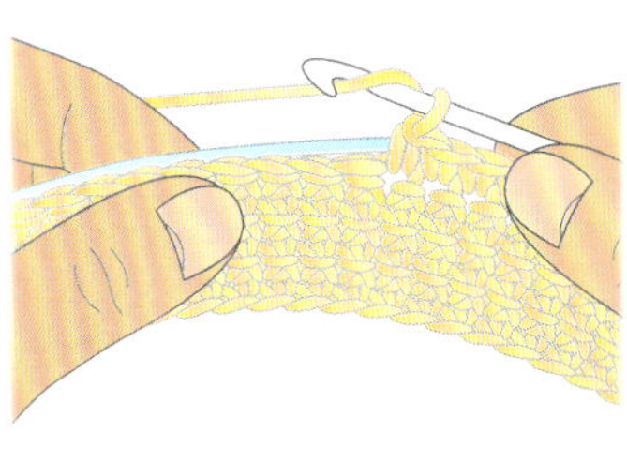

CHANGING COLOR IN SINGLE CROCHET

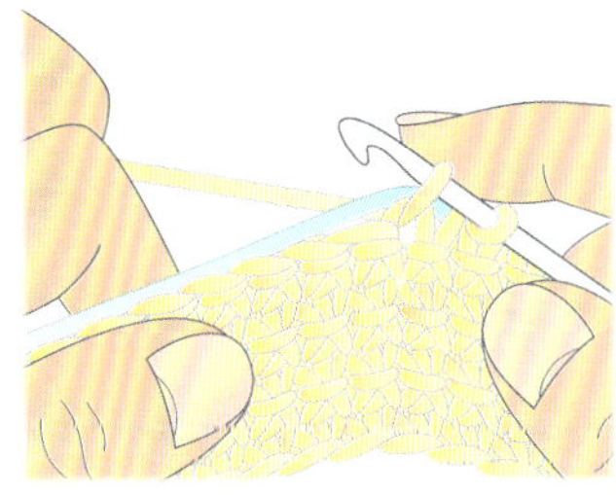

1 With the first color, pull the yarn through the next stitch, yarn over and pull through.

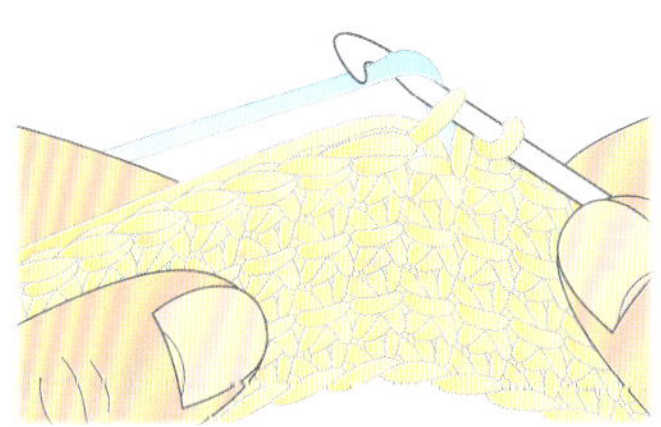

2 Using the second color, yarn over hook.

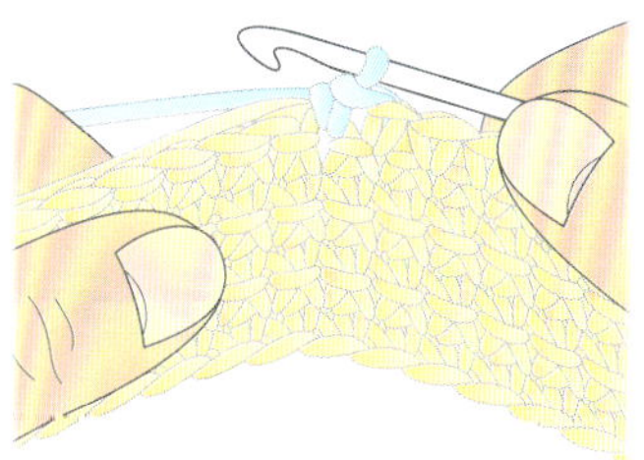

3 Pull the new color yarn through both loops on the hook to complete the stitch and change to the new color. Continue in the second color, working over the first color.

TURNING AT THE END OF A ROW

1 With the working color, make the appropriate length turning chain. Pull the second yarn up, holding it tight along the top of your work. Work the next stitch over the second yarn, catching it behind the piece.

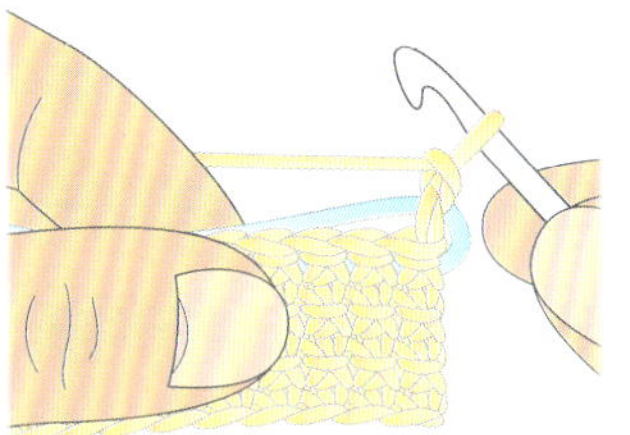

2 Continue to work over the second yarn as shown.

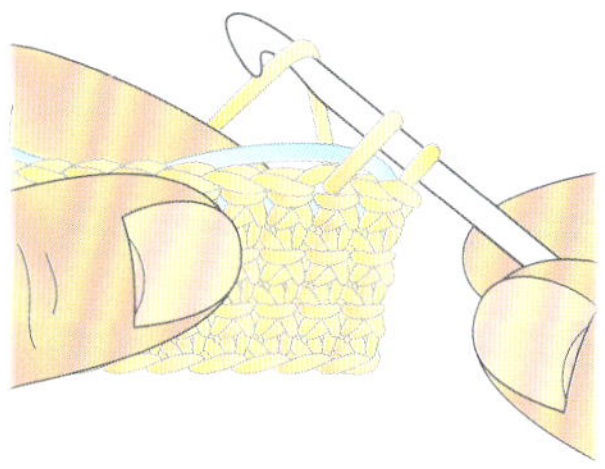

Fastening off

When you have finished crocheting, you need to fasten off the stitches to stop all your work unraveling.

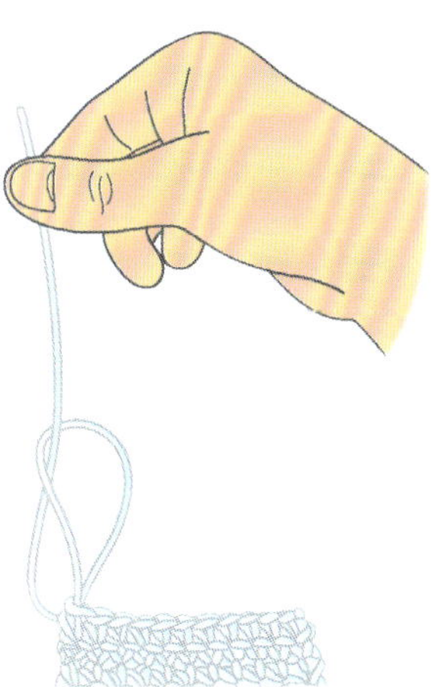

Draw up the final loop of the last stitch to make it bigger. Cut the yarn, leaving a tail of approximately 4in (10cm)—unless a longer end is needed for sewing up. Pull the tail all the way through the loop and pull the loop up tightly.

Sewing in yarn ends

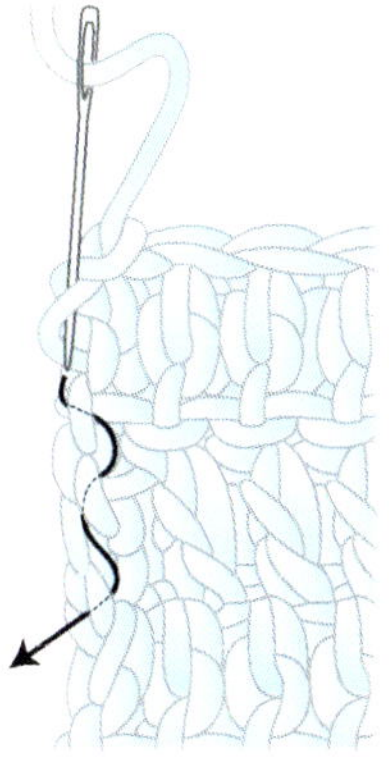

It is important to sew in the tail ends of the yarn so that they are secure and your crochet won't unravel. Thread a yarn needle with the tail end of yarn. On the wrong side, take the needle through the crochet one stitch down on the edge, then take it through the stitches, working in a gentle zigzag. Work through four or five stitches then return in the opposite direction. Remove the needle, pull the crochet gently to stretch it and trim the end.

Blocking

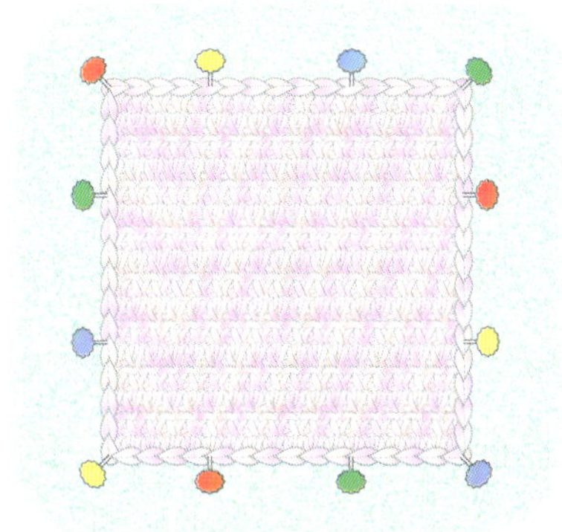

Crochet can tend to curl, so to make flat pieces stay flat you may need to block them. Pin the piece out to the correct size and shape on an ironing board or some soft foam mats (such as the ones sold as children's play mats). Spray the crochet with water and leave it to dry completely before unpinning and removing from the board or mats.

How to measure a gauge (tension) square

Using the hook and the yarn recommended in the pattern, make a number of chains to measure approximately 6in (15cm). Working in the stitch pattern given for the gauge measurements, work enough rows to form a square. Fasten off.

Take a ruler, place it horizontally across the square and, using pins, mark a 4in (10cm) area. Repeat vertically to form a 4in (10cm) square on the fabric. Count the number of stitches across, and the number of rows within the square, and compare against the gauge given in the pattern.

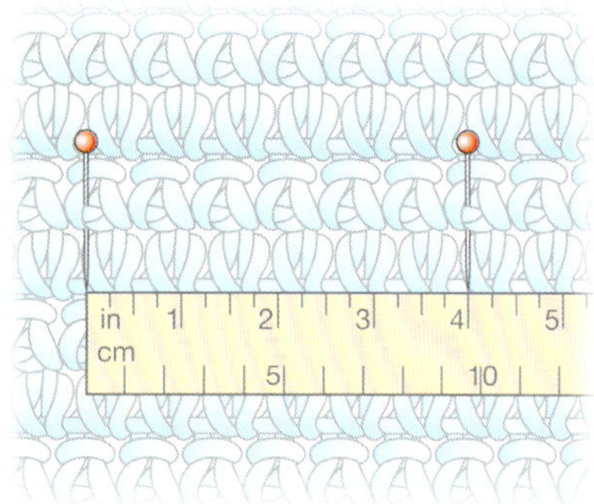

Joining squares together

MAKING A SINGLE CROCHET SEAM OR SLIP STITCH SEAM

With a single crochet seam you join two pieces together using a crochet hook and working a single crochet stitch through both pieces, instead of sewing them together with a tail of yarn and a yarn sewing needle. This makes a quick and strong seam and gives a slightly raised finish to the edging. For a less raised seam, follow the same basic technique, but work each stitch in slip stitch rather than single crochet.

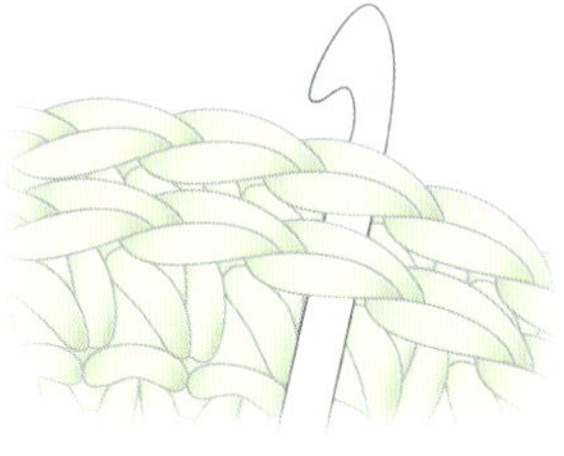

1 Start by lining up the two pieces with wrong sides together. Insert the hook in the top 2 loops of the stitch of the first piece, then into the corresponding stitch on the second piece.

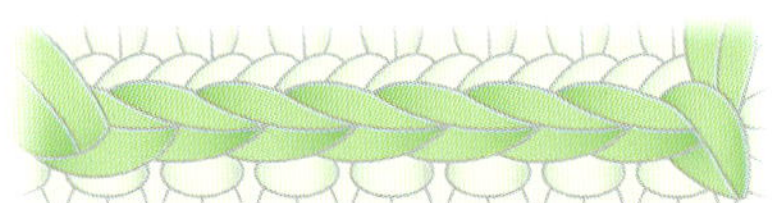

2 Complete the single crochet stitch as normal and continue on the next stitches as directed in the pattern. This gives a raised effect if the single crochet stitches are made on the right side of the work.

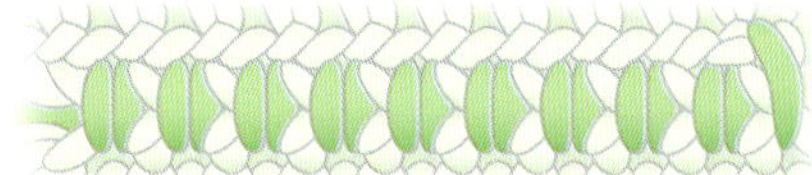

3 You can work with the wrong side of the work facing (with the pieces right side facing) if you don't want this effect and it still creates a good strong join.

MAKING AN OVERSEWN SEAM

An oversewn join gives a nice flat seam and is the simplest and most common joining technique.

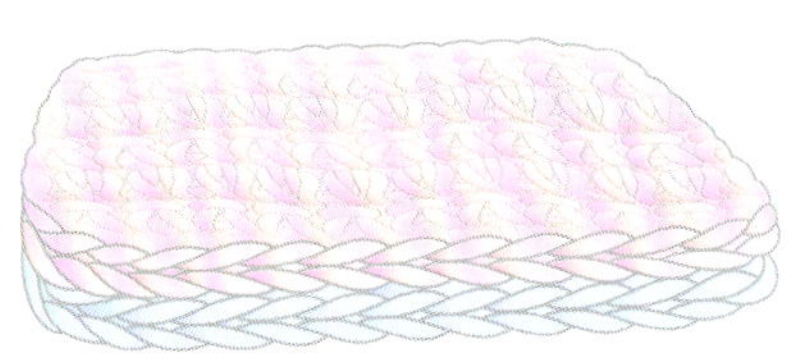

1 Thread a yarn sewing needle with the yarn you're using in the project. Place the pieces to be joined with right sides together.

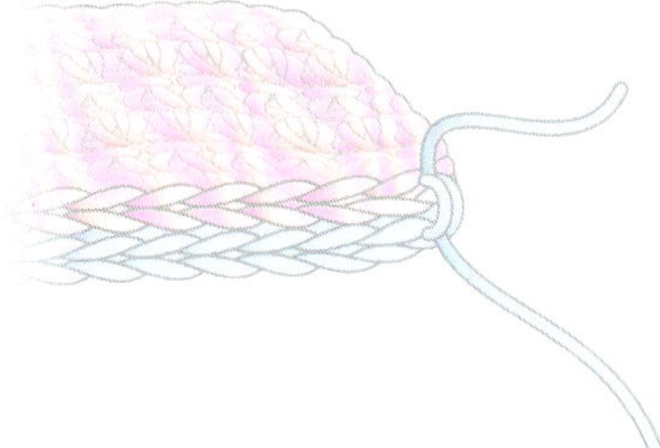

2 Insert the needle in one corner in the top loops of the stitches of both pieces and pull up the yarn, leaving a tail of about 2in (5cm). Go into the same place with the needle and pull up the yarn again; repeat two or three times to secure the yarn at the start of the seam.

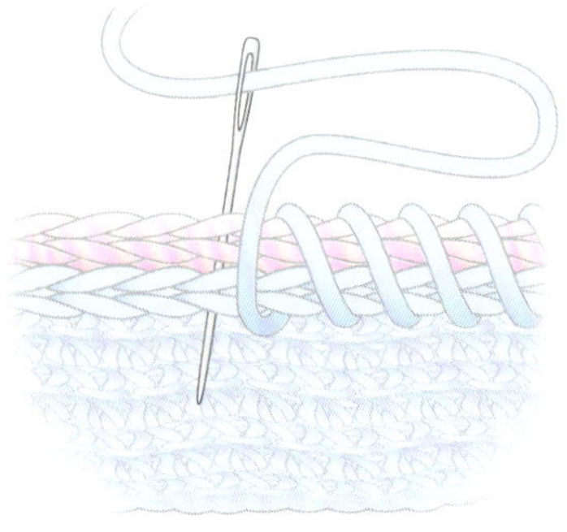

3 Join the pieces together by taking the needle through the loops at the top of corresponding stitches on each piece to the end. Fasten off the yarn at the end, as in step 2.

Bobble

Bobbles are created when working on wrong-side rows and the bobble is then pushed out toward the right-side row. This is a four-double crochet cluster bobble (4dcCL), and it shows the general technique for making bobbles. The bobbles in the patterns are worked in slightly different ways—make sure you follow the exact instructions in the pattern.

1 Yarn over hook and then insert the hook in the stitch, yarn over hook and pull the yarn through the work.

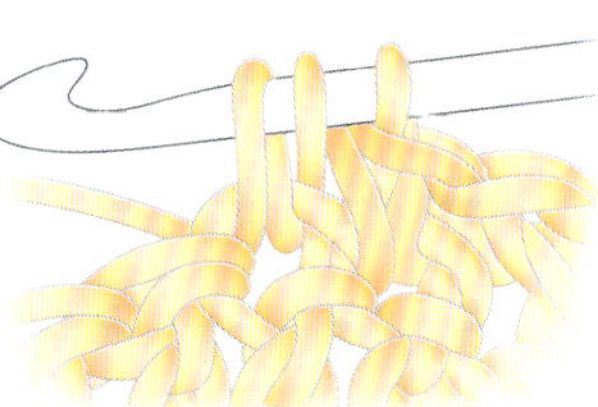

2 Yarn over hook and pull the yarn through the first 2 loops on the hook (2 loops on hook).

3 Repeat steps 1 and 2 three more times in the same stitch, yarn over hook and pull through all 5 loops on the hook.

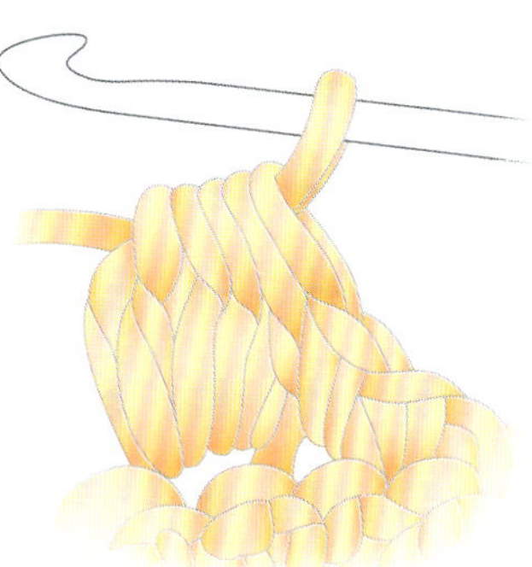

4 You can also make 1 chain to complete the bobble.

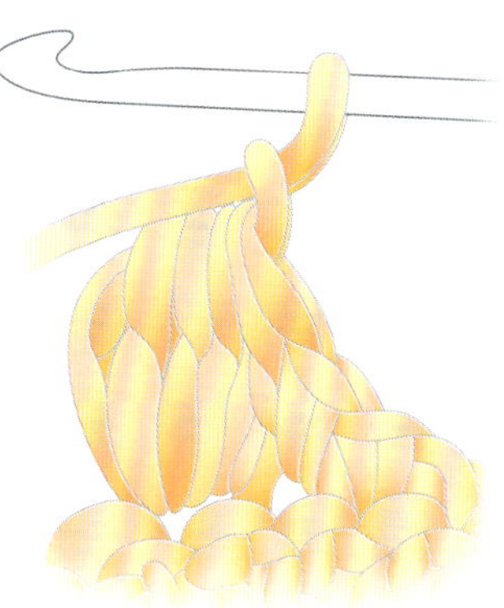

Picots

A picot is a little bobble texture that is often used to create decorative little points along the outer edge of an edging. This sample shows how to make a 3ch-picot, but follow the instructions in the pattern for the number of chains to make.

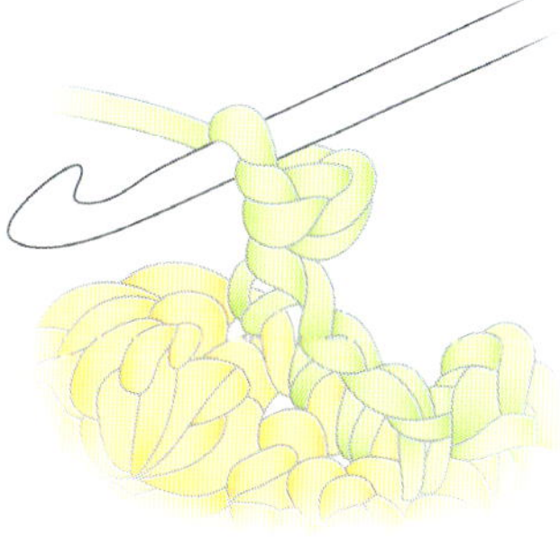

1 Make 14ch.
Row 1: 1sc in second ch from hook, 1sc in each ch to end.
Row 2: 1ch, 1sc in each of next 2 sts, 3dc in next st, *1sc in each of the next 3 sts, 3dc in next st, rep from * twice more, 2sc in each of last 2 sts.
Row 3 (picot row): 1ch, 1sc in each of next 2 sc, 1sc in top of next dc, *3ch.

2 Sl st in third ch from hook (one picot made), 1sc in top of next dc.

3 Rep from * once more, 3ch, sl st in third ch from hook (picot made)**, 1sc in each of next 3 sc, 1sc in top of next dc, rep from * ending last rep at **, 1sc in each of last two sc.

Loop stitch

1 With the yarn over your left index finger, insert the hook into the next stitch and draw two strands through the stitch (take the first strand from under the index finger and at the same time take the second strand from over the index finger).

2 Pull the yarn to tighten the loop, forming a 1in (2.5cm) loop on the index finger. Remove your finger from the loop, put the loop to the back of the work, yarn over hook and pull through three loops on the hook (1 loop stitch made on the back of the work).

Surface crochet

Surface crochet is a simple way to add extra decoration to a finished item, working slip stitches over the surface of the fabric.

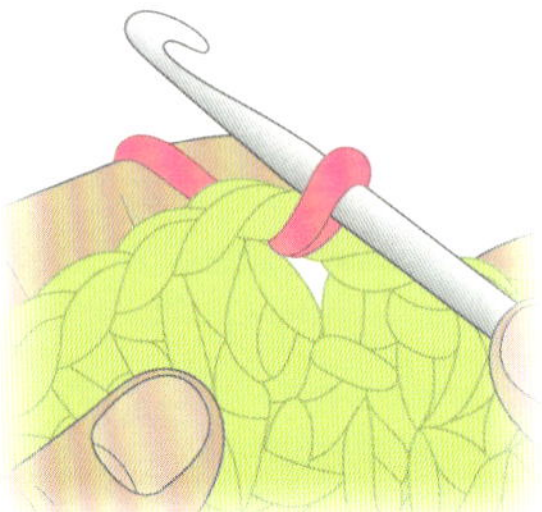

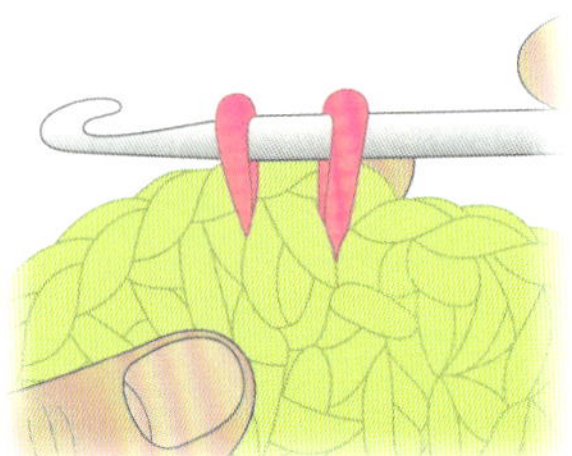

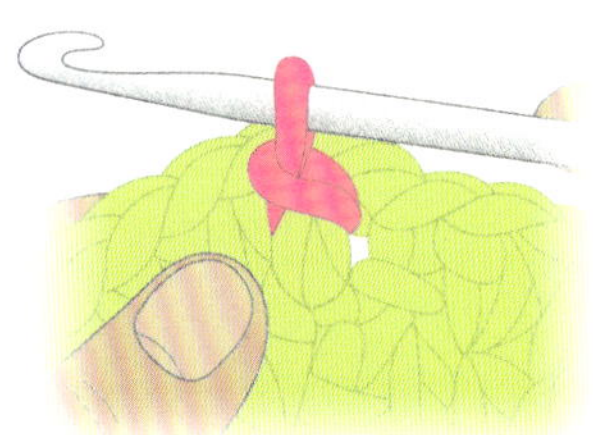

1 Using a contrast yarn, make a slip knot (see page 116). Holding the yarn with the slip knot behind the work and the hook in front, insert the hook between two stitches from front to the back and catch the slip knot behind the work with the hook. Draw the slip knot back through, so there is 1 loop on the hook at the front of the work.

2 Insert the hook between the next 2 stitches, yarn over hook, and draw a loop through to the front. You will now have 2 loops on the hook.

3 Pull the first loop on the hook through the second loop to complete the first slip stitch on the surface of the work.

Repeat steps 2 and 3 to make the next slip stitch. To join two ends with an invisible join, cut the yarn and thread onto a yarn needle. Insert the needle up through the last stitch, into the first stitch as if you were crocheting it, then into the back loop of the previous stitch. Fasten off on the wrong side.

Single crochet border

Adding an edging neatens up the sides of crochet, and it can also be used to make a frame in a contrasting color to create a good effect. A single crochet border usually starts at a corner and you will be instructed in the pattern where to join the yarn. It's usually worked on the right side of the work. There are usually 2 or 3 stitches made in the corner to create the corner shape, then you make single crochet stitches along the edge to the next corner, and so on until you have worked around the whole piece. When you are working along the sides it's not always obvious where to place your hook or how to place the stitches evenly. A good method is to use either pin or stitch markers, placing them at the halfway and quarter points, then divide the number of stitches required along the edge into four so that as you get to each marker you know you have placed the stitches evenly. At the end of the round, join the first and last stitches with a slip stitch.

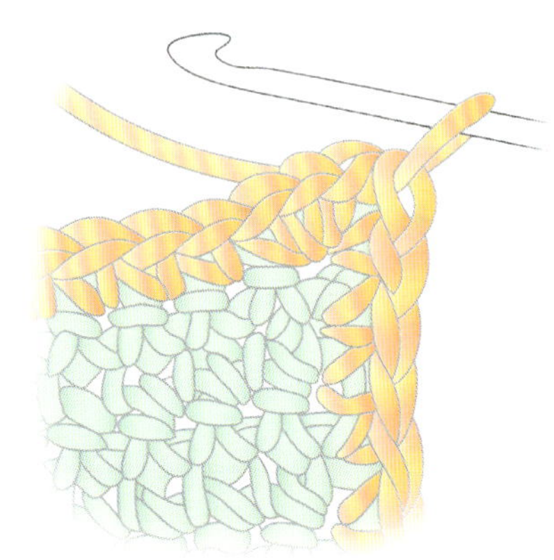

Embroidery

These decorative hand-sewing techniques are used to add details to some of the projects.

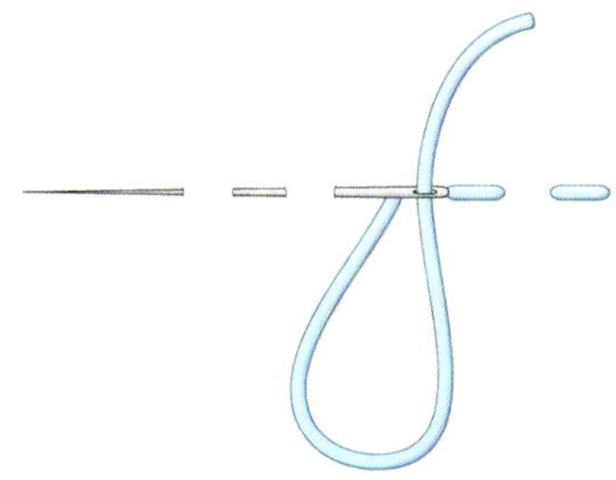

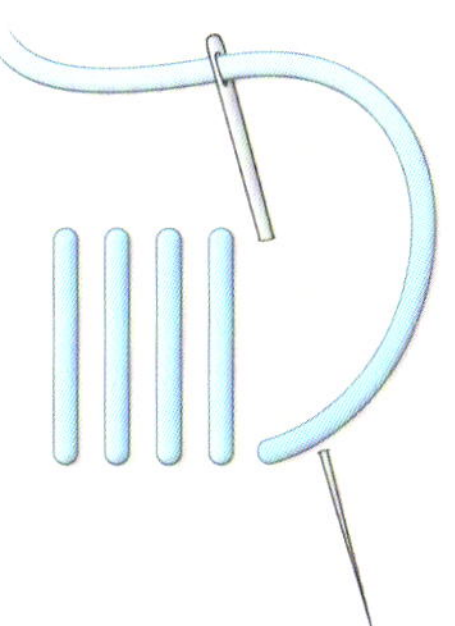
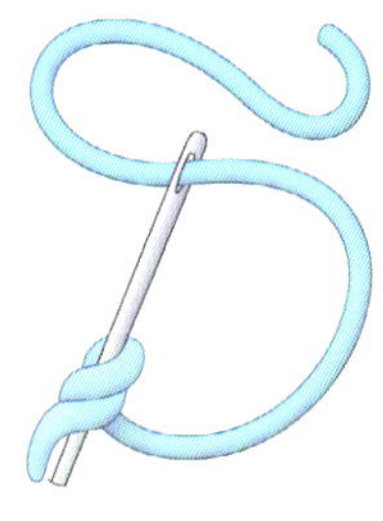

RUNNING STITCH

Bring the needle to the surface of the fabric and take it back down to the left of the entry point, to create a straight stitch. Bring the needle back to the surface a stitch length away from the last stitch and return through the fabric as before. Continue to create stitches of equal length.

STRAIGHT STITCH

Bring the needle through to the surface of the fabric and then take it back down to create a small straight stitch. These can be worked at different lengths and angles to create a variety of effects.

FRENCH KNOTS

Bring the needle up to the surface at the position of the knot. Holding the embroidery floss (thread) taut, wrap it two or three times around the tip of the needle. Continue holding the embroidery floss under gauge as you pass the needle back down through the fabric close to the entry point. The embroidery floss will pull through the wraps and they will form a knot that sits on the surface of the fabric.

Making a wreath

There are a wide range of wreaths available to buy, either online, in hobby stores, or from a florist's, but it's also easy to make your own. For a wreath approximately 12in (30cm) in diameter when finished, you will need two 1¾oz (50g) packs of raffia and a roll of florist's wire. This method gives a very lightweight base that can be moulded to the shape that you want. Raffia can be purchased either online or from hobby stores and it comes in a range of different colors.

Begin by taking the lengths of raffia out of the packets and carefully teasing the strands into long, straight lengths. Take one of the lengths and carefully attach the florist's wire tightly around one end to secure it. Begin twisting the raffia and the wire together, working your way down the length of raffia and wrapping the wire tightly around it as you twist.

As you work your way along the raffia, you will find that it will become a little thinner as you get toward the end of the strand. At this point, bring in the next length of raffia and carry on in the same way until you have combined both lengths of raffia into one long length. Add extra wire if there are parts that seem to need extra support. Trim all along the length of raffia to neaten, then secure the ends together with florist's wire to make a ring shape.

When attaching the crochet elements to your wreath, it's best to use a hot glue gun.

Hanging garlands and wreaths

Hanging up a garland or displaying a wreath is such a quick way to add an instant change to your home décor, whether it's to welcome in a new season or to add decoration for festivals and celebrations. Garlands work particularly well hung below a mantelpiece or shelf, whether it's above a fireplace, in a bedroom or even in the kitchen. They work equally well strung along bannisters of a staircase—and if you are lucky enough to have a house full of beams, the world is your oyster! Wreaths are very versatile and can be hung anywhere and everywhere, from a wall, to a door, to a gate. They also work equally well as stand-alone ornaments positioned on a shelf, mantelpiece or dressing table.

I find the best way to secure a garland is by attaching a small hanging loop, made with either string or thin wire, at the back at each end. If your garland is divided into swags, just add further loops where needed to support the shape.

The hanging loop for a wreath can be hidden away at the back by attaching a loop of string or wire. Alternatively, the loop can be very much a part of the design, perhaps worked in coordinating ribbon and big enough to be seen over the top of the wreath.

STORAGE

Wreaths and garlands can be stored by wrapping them in acid-free tissue paper and carefully packing them into a box.

How to use and display crochet squares

For a neat bottom edge to each square, rather than working the first row into the front of the initial chain, tilt the chain slightly toward you—you will see bumps at the back of the chain (see page 116). By working into the bumps instead of the front of the chain you will create a more solid, neater starting edge.

Blocking your finished squares (see page 121) will make all the difference to your work. If your square is not regularly shaped, blocking will enable you to create a perfect square.

For each square, I have also detailed how the individual pieces are attached to the finished square, either by stitching them on with a sewing needle and thread or sticking them on using a hot glue gun. When adding smaller pieces, such as attaching leaves to the wreaths, I found a pair of tweezers to be very helpful. I also found it useful to have a pack of water-soluble colored pencils to add shade and color where needed. Once made very slightly wet, the pencil works like a watercolor paint on the yarn.

FRAMED PICTURES AND COLLAGES

When framed, the festive squares serve as lovely decorations and a permanent memory of a special occasion. As most of the squares feature a slightly three-dimensional aspect, the best frames to use are box frames, as these allow for the extra depth that the squares will have. You can also pair several picture squares together in one collage box. For example, a 12in (30cm) square box frame with four 4 x 4in (10 x 10cm) mounts would work excellently with the square projects in this book.

CHRISTMAS CARDS

Any of the squares in this book lend themselves perfectly to being made into cards, such as the one on page 88. Each individual square can be stuck onto a tri-fold card blank and sent through the post. Tri-fold card blanks are readily available from craft shops or online and usually come with an envelope. I found the best way to attach the squares to the card is to use a hot glue gun as this gives a really good bond to hold the square in place.

GARLANDS

A crocheted garland is a simple yet lovely way to display your work, as the squares can be stitched onto a length of cord, ribbon or string. To stretch the bunting out if needed, you can alternate the picture squares with plain squares, worked to the same pattern as the picture square bases.

BLANKETS AND PILLOWS

Another way that the squares can be used is in larger crocheted blanket and pillow projects. For example, you can piece the festive squares together to create a patchwork pillow or blanket. Have a go at pairing them with extra squares crocheted using the same pattern as the picture square bases in a complementary color to keep the continuity. They will fit together neatly once joined, either by stitching or crocheting the seams together (see page 122). Alternatively, if you have made a plain crochet baby blanket but wish to personalize it a little, you could stitch one of the squares on as a decorative motif.

Abbreviations

approx.	approximately
beg	beginning
BLO	back loop only
ch	chain
cont	continu(e)ing
dc	double crochet
FLO	front loop only
hdc	half double crochet
MB	make bobble
PM	place marker
rem	remain(ing)
rep	repeat
RS	right side
sc	single crochet
sc2tog	single crochet 2 stitches together
sl st	slip stitch
sp(s)	space(s)
tog	together
tr	treble
WS	wrong side
yoh	yarn over hook
*	repeat sequence from * number of times stated
( )	work stitches inside brackets all into same stitch or space stated
[ ]	work sequence inside square brackets number of times stated

Crochet stitch conversion chart

Crochet stitches are worked in the same way in both the USA and the UK, but the stitch names are not the same and identical names are used for different stitches. Below is a list of the US terms used in this book, and the equivalent UK terms.

US TERM	UK TERM
single crochet (sc)	double crochet (dc)
half double crochet (hdc)	half treble (htr)
double crochet (dc)	treble (tr)
treble (tr)	double treble (dtr)
gauge	tension
yarn over hook (yoh)	yarn over hook (yoh)

Suppliers

We cannot cover all stockists here, so please explore the local yarn shops and online retailers in your own country. If you wish to substitute a different yarn for the one recommended in the pattern, try the Yarnsub website for suggestions: www.yarnsub.com.

Etsy
Square aperture card blanks and 3-D box photo frames
I used the square aperture tri-fold card blanks (5-pack, 16 colors or mixed pack, 4¾in/12cm square card with 3½in/9cm window) from HandycraftTime, and a 3-D box photo frame (5in/12.5cm square in Natural) from NIFrames Direct.

USA

LoveCrafts
Yarns and craft supplies
www.lovecrafts.com

Knitting Fever Inc.
Yarn, hooks
www.knittingfever.com

WEBS
Yarn, hooks
www.yarn.com

Michaels
Craft supplies
www.michaels.com

AUSTRALIA

Sunspun
Yarn, hooks
Tel: +61 (0)3 9830 1609
www.sunspun.com.au

UK

LoveCrafts
Yarns and craft supplies
www.lovecrafts.com

Wool
Yarn, hooks
+44 (0)1225 469144
www.woolbath.co.uk

Wool Warehouse
Yarns and craft supplies
www.woolwarehouse.co.uk

VV Rouleaux
Ribbons and rope cord
+44 (0)207 627 4455
www.vvrouleaux.com

Laughing Hens
Yarn, hooks
Tel: +44 (0)1829 740903
www.laughinghens.com

John Lewis
Craft supplies
www.johnlewis.com

Hobbycraft
Yarns and craft supplies
www.hobbycraft.co.uk

Acknowledgments

Thank you to the amazing team at CICO Books and MAKEetc, who have once again allowed me to create a crochet book that I couldn't be prouder of. I am so grateful for their faith in me and for allowing me to make my crochet dreams become reality. It is always so exciting when the first photos start to come back through showing my designs so beautifully styled and photographed.

Index